W. C. F. HARTLEY is an Assistant Director of Management Development Programmes at the University of Bradford Management Center, England.

YALE L. MELTZER is Adjunct Assistant Professor of Finance at Pace University, New York City.

Cash Management

Planning, Forecasting, and Control

W. C. F. HARTLEY AND YALE L. MELTZER

A SPECTRUM BOOK

PRENTICE-HALL, INC., Englewood Cliffs, New Jersey 07632

106064

0553811

Library of Congress Cataloging in Publication Data

HARTLEY, W C F
    Cash management.

    (A Spectrum Book)
    Published in 1976 under title: Cash.
    Includes index.
    1. Cash management. 2. Cash flow. I. Meltzer,
Yale L., joint author. II. Title.
HG4028.C45H37 1979   658.1$'$5244   79-11379
ISBN 0-13-120295-2
ISBN 0-13-120287-1 pbk.

Editorial/production supervision and interior design by Carol Smith
Cover design by Judith Kazdym Leeds
Manufacturing buyer: Cathie Lenard

Originally published as *Cash: Planning, Forecasting and Control* by
Business Books Limited, London, England.

© 1979 by Prentice-Hall, Inc., *Englewood Cliffs, New Jersey 07632*

All rights reserved. No part of this book may be reproduced in any form
or by any means without permission in writing from the publisher.

A SPECTRUM BOOK

10 9 8 7 6 5 4 3 2 1

Printed in the United States of America

PRENTICE-HALL INTERNATIONAL, INC., *London*
PRENTICE-HALL OF AUSTRALIA PTY. LIMITED, *Sydney*
PRENTICE-HALL OF CANADA, LTD., *Toronto*
PRENTICE-HALL OF INDIA PRIVATE LIMITED, *New Delhi*
PRENTICE-HALL OF JAPAN, INC., *Tokyo*
PRENTICE-HALL OF SOUTHEAST ASIA PTE. LTD., *Singapore*
WHITEHALL BOOKS LIMITED, *Wellington, New Zealand*

Contents

v

~~106064~~

055381)

vi

Preface

We have written this book for both non-financial and financial managers to attempt both to clarify the role and behavior of cash flow within a firm and to suggest a practical means for forecasting and controlling cash flow. We do not see cash forecasting and control as a purely financial responsibility. It is a team effort, but we believe that the ultimate responsibility for both cash forecasting and cash control rests with non-financial, operating managers; it is they who exercise those judgments and initiate those operating decisions that represent the major determinants of cash flow. We hope this book will help them become more aware of the significance of cash flow to a firm, what is involved in forecasting cash movements, and the scope for control of cash flows.

This is not to say that financial managers play only a passive role in the operation: clearly they must provide whatever backup computational assistance is required by operating management, and accountants and other people responsible for producing a cash forecast or cash control information should find something to help them gain an overview of what is involved and acquire greater confidence to tackle or overhaul the job in their own firms.

Since we believe that our subject is essentially practical and more for "doers" than "thinkers," we have tried to make the content as practical as possible. We have suggested several forms that, amended to meet the requirements of your own situation, might provide the basis for an administrative framework around which to develop an operationally acceptable approach to cash forecasting and control in an individual firm. Chapter 1 discusses some basic matters about the behavior of cash flow. Chapter 2 sets down a framework for analysis. In Chapters 3 through 6, we examine the practice of forecasting, monitoring, and controlling cash flow over both the short and long term.

The first six chapters conclude with a continuing case study of a fictitious company that demonstrates how each chapter's content has been adapted and applied in one specific case; ideally, you should tackle each part of this study where it appears before moving on to the next chapter. We invite you to try producing the necessary information and presentation format and later on to compare your views with ours. Chapters 7 and 8 review forecasting in an uncertain environment and reacting quickly to a developing financial emergency, two crucial matters of particularly practical importance with which all managers must learn to live.

We have an unshakable faith in management's resilience and ability to react to any environmental changes that may be forced upon it. Without doubt, a greater awareness of cash and the ability to live with the twin problems of liquidity and inflation are *de rigueur* as we write. We hope that what we have written will be of assistance in this respect.

Cash
Management

1

Cash Flow
in Perspective

This book is about cash flow. Cash is a very simple concept
and yet its importance to the ability of the firm
to continue in existence is without question.
Cash flow is the lifeblood of business:
without it the firm dies,
as many, both large and small, have done
and unhappily will continue to do.
And yet, despite its simplicity, cash flow is very often
not fully understood or appreciated by management.
Let us therefore begin this book
by examining just what cash flow is,
what makes it behave in the way it does
and what scope there is
for management control over cash flow.

1.1 IMPORTANCE OF CASH

If asked to state the ultimate objective of business existence, many managers would variously suggest that it must be "to make a profit" or "to stay in business" and indeed in the long term these two things are very much one and the same. To be more specific: if a firm is to continue in existence over the long term it must generate income sufficiently in excess of current expenditure to provide for replacement of its assets, improved standards of employment for its employees, an adequate return to shareholders and additionally a further amount over and above to provide for growth of the business in an inflationary environment. Survival and growth in the long term therefore rely upon the continued generation of an adequate after-tax profit. Little wonder, therefore, that long-term objectives or growth plans incorporate some reference to profit. But does it follow that profit shall also be the objective in the short term? The answer is yes and no: on the one hand it must be just as necessary to make a profit in the

3

short term as it is in the long term; however, there is a more pressing need in the short term which is not necessarily the same thing as making a profit. The short-term need is simply to stay in business—to avoid bankruptcy. Management must ensure that the firm at least stays out of bankruptcy in the short term if it is to live to enjoy the fruits of profit in the long term.

Bankruptcy occurs when a firm runs out of cash and is thus unable to meet its debts when they are due for payment, i.e. when cash inflows are not of sufficient amount or do not come in sufficient time to meet necessary cash out-flows. Bankruptcy is, of course, the end, but short of bankruptcy, a firm could suffer acute cash inadequacy and be forced thereby to accept quite considerable constraints upon its freedom of action. Cash inadequacy is clearly not as disas-trous as bankruptcy but is nevertheless equally critical to the firm. The object of cash management is thus to ensure that cash inflows are available in the right amount *and at the right time* to meet obligatory cash outflows. It is as simply stated as that. And yet still firms go bankrupt!

It is difficult to isolate one single cause for mismanagement of cash but without doubt a frequent contributory factor arises from concern for the long-term need for profit discussed above. It is the naive belief that profits and cash are somehow the same thing: in other words, the mistaken belief that, if a firm makes a profit, this will automatically be reflected by an identical increase in the amount in the cash till. Unfortunately this is not the case: profitable firms have been known to go bankrupt whereas firms sustaining losses have been known to have a cash till overflow with surplus funds. So let us begin by establishing the difference between profit flows on the one hand and cash flows on the other. Ability to establish the difference will enable us to be aware of some potential dangers or problem areas and also to highlight items that must receive particular attention when forecasting or controlling cash flow. It can all be summarized in the trite, but nevertheless, true statement that "Profit is an opinion but cash is a fact."

1.2 PROFIT VERSUS CASH FLOW

Profit, as measured by the accountant, is a technical expression that represents the excess of current income over current expenditures. Such income and ex-penditures are not necessarily cash inflows and cash outflows—they are the result of the consistent application of traditional accounting principles of relevance and conservatism from one accounting period to another. When determining profit, the accountant seeks to apply basic rules which will produce conservative estimates of those incomes and expenditures that are deemed relevant to the accounting period under review, irrespective of whether or not they have been received or paid in cash. What is relevant and whether it is adequately conservative must obviously require the expression of opinion by the accountant. It is thus quite fair to observe that profit is not a fact but an opinion—albeit an opinion reflecting the accumulated expertise of a professionally qualified accountant.

Profit is a complex concept as the brief statement above will confirm. To thoroughly explain the concept would require a much fuller discussion but fortunately this book is not about profit; it is about cash flow: cash is a much more simple concept and therefore easier to explain. Cash flow is the difference between the actual cash flowing into and out of the cash till or bank account. That is not an opinion but a hard fact!

A few simple examples will demonstrate application of the main accounting principles of profit measurement and will help to explain the main causes of disparity between profit flows and cash flows.

1.2.1 Capital Expenditure and Depreciation

Capital expenditure represents the acquisition of a physical item of a long-lasting nature such as plant, equipment or motor vehicles. Because the item will last for several years, the accounting concept of relevance does not charge the cost of the item against profits in the year of acquisition but seeks to spread its cost in some equitable manner against profits over its estimated useful working life. This act of spreading is called depreciation. Profit is thus arrived at after charging depreciation. On the other hand, as far as the cash till is concerned, there is an immediate outflow as soon as the item is acquired and payment made. From this brief description three facts emerge:

1 Cash flow from operations is basically profit before charging depreciation.

2 In any year in which capital expenditure is incurred, the total cash flow of the firm could be negative despite having made a profit.

3 In any year in which there is no capital expenditure, the total cash flow will be higher than profit by the amount of the depreciation charge.

A simple demonstration will illustrate these facts.

Mr. B. Arrow buys and sells fruit for cash and his only other expenses are his personal wages. In his first year's trading he also buys a barrow from which to sell his fruit for $300, which has an estimated useful working life of five years. The result of his operations

	Year 1 $	Year 2 $	Year 3 $	Year 4 $	Year 5 $
Cash purchases	600	600	500	600	600
Cash wages	500	500	500	500	500
Total cash expenses	1100	1100	1000	1100	1100
Cash sales	1200	1200	1050	1050	1200
Cash flow from operations	100	100	50	(50)	100
Depreciation, $300 ÷ 5yrs	60	60	60	60	60
Profit (loss)	$40	$40	($10)	($110)	$40
Cash flow from operations	100	100	50	(50)	100
Capital expenditure	(300)	-	-	-	-
Total cash flow	($200)	$100	$50	($50)	$100

Brackets indicate negatives. Notice also that:
1 The cash flow from operations each year is the profit before charging depreciation.
2 In Year 1 the total cash flow is negative $200, despite the profit of $40.
3 In Years 2 to 5, total cash flow is always higher than the profit by $60 - the amount of the depreciation charge.

Figure 1.1

over the five years, expressed both in profit (or loss) terms and in cash flow terms are as shown in Figure 1.1.

1.2.2 Inventories, i.e. Stock and Work-in-Progress

When computing profit, the relevance concept of accounting will normally deduct the cost of inventory only at the time it is sold. However, as far as the cash till is concerned, there is an immediate outflow as soon as the inventory is acquired and paid for. It therefore follows that:

4 In any accounting period during which the value of unsold inventories increases, there will be a cash outflow which will not be reflected by a reduction in profits.

5 In any accounting period during which the value of unsold inventories decreases, there will be a cash inflow which will not be reflected by an increase in profits. For example:

Mr. B. Arrow buys "Plods" for $3 each and sells them for $5 each, always for cash and incurring no other expenses (see Figure 1.2).

	Period 1	Period 2	Period 3
Buy for cash	10	7	7
Sell for cash	8	8	8
Closing inventory	2	1	-
	$	$	$
Computation of profit:			
Opening inventory	-	6	3
Purchases for cash ($3 each)	30	21	21
	30	27	24
Closing inventory ($3 each)	6	3	-
Cost of goods sold ($3 each)	24	24	24
Sales for cash ($5 each)	40	40	40
Profit: $2 on each item sold	$16	$16	$16
Computation of cash flow:			
Sales for cash	40	40	40
Purchases for cash	(30)	(21)	(21)
Net cash flow	$10	$19	$19

Notice that:
4 In Period 1 the net cash flow is lower than the profit by
   $6 - the amount of the increase in value of inventory.
5 In Periods 2 and 3 the net cash flow is higher than the
   profit by $3 - the amount of the decrease in value of
   inventory

Figure 1.2

1.2.3 Credit Trading

When computing profit, the relevance concept of accounting will admit income and expenditures at the invoice stage and indeed sometimes even before if delivery has already taken place. However, as far as the cash till is concerned, the cash inflow or outflow will frequently take place much later on expiration of normal credit terms. This can have a considerable impact upon the difference between profit and cash flows as a further example from our hypothetical "Plod" business will reveal (still buying at $3 and selling for $5)—see Figure 1.3. It is clear

Figure 1.3

Period		Profit, $	Net cash flow, $	Amount still owing on Sales, $	Amount still owing on Purchases, $
4	Buy 10 for cash, sell 10 for cash	20	20	Nil	Nil
5	Buy 10 for cash, sell 10 on credit	20	(30)	(50)	
6	Buy 10 on credit, sell 10 for cash	20	50		30
7	Buy 10 on credit, sell 10 on credit	20	Nil	(50)	30

from this further example that an extension of credit to customers is equivalent to an outflow of cash in that it delays cash inflow: see Period 5 where the profit (and hence the cash flow from operations) of $20 is reduced to a final cash flow of negative $30 due to the $50 extension of credit to customers. Similarly, Period 6 reveals that an extension of credit from suppliers is equivalent to an inflow of cash in that it delays cash outflow. Our brief excursion into the principles of profit measurement and the main causes of disparity between profit flows and cash flows can now be rounded out by the following further observations:

6 In any accounting period during which there is an increase in the amount of credit extended to customers (known in accounting parlance as debtors, or accounts receivable, or receivables), cash flow from operations will in effect be reduced by this amount.

7 In any accounting period during which there is an increase in the amount of credit taken from suppliers (known in accounting parlance as creditors, or accounts payable, or payables), cash flow from operations will in effect be increased by this amount.

Let us conclude this brief survey of the causes of disparity between profit flows and cash flows with a final example which puts together many of the seven observations above and so demonstrates their combined effect when several of the causes occur simultaneously:

Flush with the success of his earlier business venture, our friend Mr. B. Arrow decides to purchase a second barrow for $20 which he expects to last for four years and from which he intends to sell "Plods" exclusively as a separate business enterprise. During his first year he buys sixteen "Plods" at $3 each, one of which is still to be paid for at the end of the year. During the year he sells twelve "Plods" at $5 each but again, due to selling on credit, he is still owed for two at the end of the year. Because Mr. Arrow is occupied on his first barrow he puts a manager in charge of the new venture and pays him a salary of $16 during this first year of operation. For Mr. Arrow's first accounting period of one year, the profit statement shown in Figure 1.4 would reveal the income, expenditure, and profit deemed to be relevant to the period. On the other hand Mr. Arrow's cash or bank account would read as shown in Figure 1.5 for the same period. Thus, despite having made a profit of $3, Mr. Arrow has experienced a considerably negative cash flow. This can be explained as shown in Figure 1.6.

	$	$
Sale of Plods (12 & $5)		60
Less: Cost of Plods sold (12 @ $3)	36	
Salary paid to manager	16	
Depreciation ($20 ÷ 4 years)	5	57
Profit from operations		$3

Figure 1.4

	$	$
Cash collections from customers		
(12 sold less 2 still owing = 10 @ $5)		50
Cash payments to suppliers		
(16 bought less 1 still owing = 15 & $3)	45	
Salary paid to manager in cash	16	
Cash paid for new barrow	20	81
Net cash *deficit*		$31

Figure 1.5

		Inflow of cash, $	Outflow of cash, $
1	Cash flow from operations, i.e. profit before charging depreciation*	8	
2	Purchase of new barrow		20
4	Increase in inventory of Plod, i.e. 16 purchased less 12 sold = 4 @ $3 each		12
6	Extension of credit to customers, i.e. still owed for 2 @ $5		10
7	Extension of credit from suppliers, i.e. still owing for 1 @ $3	3	
Total impact of operations on cash flow		$11	$42
Therefore, net impact on cash flow = deficit		$31	
*Henceforth strictly referred to as *potential* cash flow from operations because if the customers do not pay to Mr Arrow the $10 they owe then operations will not have provided a positive cash flow at all.			

Figure 1.6

1.3 IMPACT OF GROWTH ON CASH FLOW

From the seven observations in Section 1.2 it is hoped that the reader might begin to appreciate some of the causes of disparity between profit and total cash flow. Indeed it should be apparent that it will be nothing short of a remarkable coincidence if these two quantities are identical in amount. Moreover these causes of disparity are constantly evident during normal operations: sometimes the disparity moves in one direction, sometimes in another, hopefully balancing out over time. But let us consider the specific situation of a firm which is going through a period of rapid but profitable growth. Consider the impact of each of the seven observations in turn against the following consequences of growth. During a period of growth:

1 Capital expenditures will no doubt continue at a high level—the second observation in Section 1.2 indicates that total cash flow may therefore be negative despite profitable sales.

2 Inventories will almost certainly increase in order to meet the growing demand—the fourth observation in Section 1.2 indicates that total cash flow will thereby be reduced despite any profit made.

3 The amount of credit given to customers and taken from suppliers must both increase, but the value of the increase in debtors or receivables (being based upon sales values) is likely to exceed the value of the increase in creditors or payables (being based upon purchase values)—the sixth and seventh observations in Section 1.2 would seem to indicate again that total cash flow will thereby be reduced.

4 Finally, cash flow from operations is likely to be low because profit will no doubt be low until volume is built up and margins are established.

It is clear that a firm going through a period of rapid growth is in a particularly vulnerable position as the foregoing brief analysis reveals. Everything is working against the cash flow of the firm. No wonder that many promising firms wither and die for lack of capital. This situation is often referred to in the United Kingdom as "over trading", implying too rapid a rate of growth for the availability of capital to meet the inevitably negative cash flow.

The symptoms of too rapid a rate of growth will, to some extent, also manifest themselves in an individual product's growth. This means that a firm can find itself in a period of acute financial embarrassment if its product mix gets out of balance in such a way as to have a preponderance of products in the early stages of growth even though the firm as a whole may not be going through a total period of growth. The ideal product mix would finance the young, cash hungry, growing product out of surplus cash flows from existing mature products.

1.4 IMPACT OF INFLATION ON CASH FLOW

Section 1.3 referred to growth and its impact on cash flow. This impact was one of the impact of volume changes which were reflected in cash values. But it is the *value* not the *volume* that really counts in the cash till.

Consider now the impact of inflation during any accounting period:

1 Will not the *values* of capital expenditure continue to increase beyond the depreciation charge (which was based upon original cost of the existing assets)?

2 Will not the *values* of inventories increase irrespective of volume?

3 Must not the *value* of credit given to customers exceed that taken from suppliers?

So where is the difference between growth and inflation? *Inflation is growth* in value terms and therefore in periods of rapid inflation a firm must expect to find itself in a very similarly unfavorable cash flow position to the firm that is growing fast. Pity the firm which attempts to grow during a period of rapid inflation. In financial terms it comes dangerously close to compounding a felony!

1.5 THE TIMING OF CASH FLOW

We have seen how the application of accounting concepts to the determination of profit can create problems when analyzing the amounts of cash flow. An additional problem is presented by the *time* at which the amounts flow. Cash inflows and outflows do not always flow smoothly over a period of time. Some cash outflows do flow smoothly, e.g. monthly salaries are fairly constant from month to month. However, many cash outflows must go out in one lump rather than smoothly throughout the year: for example, electricity may be paid quarterly, dividends half yearly, taxation once per annum in the United Kingdom, typically quarterly in the United States. In a seasonal business, cash inflows from customers may be higher at one part of the year than another. Put all this together and one can very easily have three firms with an identical cash balance at the beginning and end of the year but with vastly different patterns of cash flow during the year. The three graphical cumulative cash flow profiles in Figure 1.7 show this situation. Note that in each case both the opening and the

11

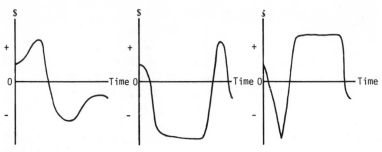

Figure 1.7

closing cash positions are identical, but each situation has a vastly different requirement for finance and availability of surplus. (Requirements appear below the horizontal axis and surpluses above). Would that cash flow always flowed in straight lines!

When we turn to the mechanics of cash forecasting, it will become vital to remember this critical time dimension to cash flow. A firm can still be in serious financial difficulty despite having a correct forecast of the amounts of cash flow if the forecast of its timing is incorrect. The reader is invited to ponder what would be the impact upon the financial position of a firm if all the firm's cash inflows, although unchanged in amount, came in three months later and simultaneously all the firm's cash outflows, similarly unchanged in amount, went out three months earlier. Or if the reader would prefer to consider something a little more cheerful: what would it be worth, in terms of bank interest saved, to bring forward by one month all the cash inflows of the firm?

Most amounts are two dimensional, namely a quantity multiplied by a price. Cash flow amounts possess the perverse third dimension of time. And indeed it is the time dimension that is at the root of the various problems created by the accounting concepts discussed above. Ultimately, over the whole life of the firm when everything has been closed down and sold off, profits and cash flow each in total from beginning to end will be identical. But this is academic because it must be assumed that the firm will not close down but will continue. Therefore in the long term "profits" must be the name of the game but in the short term cash flow is much more important.

1.6 SIGNIFICANCE OF INDUSTRIAL ENVIRONMENT

While no firm and no industry can claim to have a monopoly on cash flow problems, there are environmental constraints that can create a special brand of cash flow problem for a firm. Such problems may be created by the very nature

12

of its operations, for example the location or seasonality of the market place. A by no means exhaustive list of some typical industry problem areas follows:

1 Some aspects of retailing have the problem of a favorable cash flow position because the sales receipts are collected in cash over the counter before it becomes necessary to pay for the merchandise sold; others in retailing face the problem of collecting cash from many small customer credit accounts; still others face a considerable inventory carrying problem aggravated by seasonal sales.

2 Mail order firms have a peculiar combination of cash flow considerations: many small credit customers; many regular payments on account; high volume and wide range of inventories.

3 Travel agencies may be in the happy situation of receiving substantial deposits in advance from customers but then must live with the twin problems of substantial down payments in advance to suppliers of services and considerable foreign exchange risks.

4 Several different industries have considerable cash tied up for a long time while inventories mature, e.g. tobacco and whiskey distilling.

5 Some products are extremely short-lived and there is little time to get cash flow in balance if things begin to go wrong, e.g. "pop" records and daily newspapers.

6 The construction and building contracting industry each year produces a bumper crop of bankruptcies—perhaps because firms in the industry are involved with a relatively small number of large discrete contracts, each with a heavy initial cash outflow followed by progress payment inflows from, and retention negotiations with, clients.

7 Many firms in different industries face long, protracted settlements for large orders from overseas customers.

Every firm ought to examine its own position in order to highlight those good and bad points in its own environment which will most critically come to bear on its short-term cash flow. These are the points to which particular attention will be directed when monitoring ongoing cash flows. Figure 1.8 represents an excellent example of a presentation of financial information and data.

**GENERAL MOTORS ACCEPTANCE CORPORATION
AND SUBSIDIARIES**

ASSETS

	December 31,	
	1977	**1976**
	(In thousands of dollars)	
Cash (Note 2)	$ 342,275	$ 279,391
Marketable Securities (Note 15)		
Bonds and notes, at amortized cost (market value, 1977—$458,809 thousands; 1976—$233,539 thousands)	464,517	236,062
Stocks, at cost (market value, 1977—$115,776 thousands; 1976—$119,788 thousands)	68,193	57,526
Total marketable securities	532,710	293,588
Finance Receivables (Note 3)		
Retail	12,433,752	10,834,449
Lease financing	3,460,885	2,495,519
Leasing	28,107	18,815
Wholesale	8,140,049	6,569,208
Term loans to dealers	99,526	100,418
Accounts receivable	128,646	98,765
Total finance receivables	24,290,965	20,117,174
Deductions		
Unearned income	1,530,790	1,256,298
Allowance for financing losses (Schedule XII)	177,560	164,482
Total deductions	1,708,350	1,420,780
Finance receivables, less deductions	22,582,615	18,696,394
Other Assets		
Investment in foreign affiliate (Note 1)	18,547	13,807
Insurance receivables...	36,831	34,383
Company automobiles and office equipment, at cost less accumulated depreciation:		
1977—$22,430 thousands; 1976—$19,039 thousands..............	30,935	31,391
Unamortized debt expense	41,314	35,986
Deferred policy acquisition expense	36,972	31,945
Miscellaneous	18,474	15,299
Total other assets	183,073	162,811
Total Assets	$23,640,673	$19,432,184

Figure 1.8 Part 1

14

LIABILITIES AND STOCKHOLDER'S EQUITY

	December 31,	
	1977	1976
	(In thousands of dollars)	
Notes, Loans and Debentures Payable Within One Year (Note 4)		
Short-term notes—Commercial paper	$ 5,943,983	$ 4,925,443
—Other	3,057,241	2,374,231
Bank loans and overdrafts	606,881	512,258
Other notes, loans and debentures	871,880	793,347
Total notes, loans and debentures payable within one year	10,479,985	8,605,279
Accounts Payable and Other Liabilities		
General Motors Corporation and affiliated companies (Note 13)	2,496,581	2,173,769
Dealers (Note 5)	146,876	139,146
United States and foreign income and other taxes	114,124	100,281
Interest	197,893	146,820
Unearned insurance premiums	222,947	187,486
Insurance losses and claims	125,852	57,936
Other	91,570	75,474
Total accounts payable and other liabilities	3,395,843	2,880,912
Notes, Loans and Debentures Payable After One Year (Note 6) (Schedule IX)	6,602,102	5,201,637
Subordinated Indebtedness Payable After One Year (Note 6) (Schedule IX)	1,474,591	1,309,538
Stockholder's Equity		
Preferred stock, $100 par value (authorized and outstanding, 1,100,000 shares)		
—6% cumulative	75,000	75,000
—7¼% cumulative	35,000	35,000
Common stock, $100 par value (authorized and outstanding, 1977—7,650,000 shares; 1976—6,150,000 shares) (Note 8)	765,000	615,000
Net income retained for use in the business (Note 8)	813,152	709,818
Total stockholder's equity	1,688,152	1,434,818
Total Liabilities and Stockholder's Equity	$23,640,673	$19,432,184

Reference should be made to the Notes to Financial Statements.

Figure 1.8 Part 2

15

GENERAL MOTORS ACCEPTANCE CORPORATION
AND SUBSIDIARIES

STATEMENT OF CONSOLIDATED
INCOME AND CONSOLIDATED
NET INCOME RETAINED FOR
USE IN THE BUSINESS
FOR THE YEARS ENDED
DECEMBER 31, 1977 AND 1976

	1977	1976
	(In thousands of dollars)	
Financing Revenue		
Retail and lease financing	$1,507,418	$1,280,414
Wholesale	464,638	383,803
Total	1,972,056	1,664,217
Insurance Premiums Earned (Note 13)	342,435	239,474
Investment and Other Income*	21,320	18,563
Gross Revenue	2,335,811	1,922,254
Expenses		
Interest and discount	1,129,420	913,701
Operating expenses (Note 10)	465,098	407,282
Financing losses and loss provisions (Note 3)	69,405	68,632
Insurance losses and loss expense	261,226	201,125
United States, foreign and other income taxes (Note 11)	205,290	170,275
Total expenses	2,130,439	1,761,015
Net Income	205,372	161,239
Net Income Retained for Use in the Business at beginning of the year	709,818	625,617
Total	915,190	786,856
Cash Dividends		
Preferred stock	7,038	7,038
Common stock	95,000	70,000
Total cash dividends	102,038	77,038
Net Income Retained for Use in the Business at end of the year (Note 8)	$ 813,152	$ 709,818

*Excludes increase (decrease) in unrealized appreciation of marketable securities net of applicable income taxes .... ($ 12,505) $ 17,919

Reference should be made to the Notes to Financial Statements.

Figure 1.8   Part 3

16

GENERAL MOTORS ACCEPTANCE CORPORATION AND SUBSIDIARIES

STATEMENT OF CHANGES IN CONSOLIDATED FINANCIAL POSITION FOR THE YEARS ENDED DECEMBER 31, 1977 AND 1976

	1977	1976
	(In thousands of dollars)	
Source of Funds		
From Operations		
Net income	$ 205,372	$ 161,239
Losses and loss provisions on finance receivables (Note 3)	69,405	68,632
Depreciation (Note 10)	8,607	7,596
Increase in non-affiliated accounts payable and other liabilities	192,119	126,651
Other-net	(15,390)	(17,686)
Total from Operations	460,113	346,432
Increase in accounts payable to affiliated companies (Note 13)	322,812	534,376
Proceeds from issuance of debt		
Original maturities after one year	2,459,168	2,351,933
Original maturities within one year (net of debt repaid)	1,794,700	564,168
Proceeds from sale of common stock (Note 8)	150,000	100,000
Total	$5,186,793	$3,896,909
Application of Funds		
Increase in finance receivables (net of unearned income)	$3,955,626	$3,203,443
Repayment of debt with original maturities after one year	818,972	579,272
Cash dividends	102,038	77,038
Increase in cash and marketable securities	302,006	12,698
Purchase of fixed assets (net of disposals)	8,151	10,651
Investment in foreign affiliate	—	13,807
Total	$5,186,793	$3,896,909

Reference should be made to the Notes to Financial Statements.

Figure 1.8   Part 4

17

1. SIGNIFICANT ACCOUNTING POLICIES

Consolidation Practices: The consolidated financial statements include the accounts of the Registrant, hereinafter sometimes referred to as the "Company", and all wholly-owned domestic and foreign subsidiaries, which together with the Registrant are hereinafter sometimes referred to as "GMAC". In July 1976, the Company acquired a 51% interest in a Japanese finance company, which is accounted for on the equity method. Provisions are made, where applicable, for estimated taxes on dividends which may be paid from undistributed profits of subsidiaries and affiliates.

Unearned Finance Income: In the case of notes receivable in which the face amount includes the finance charge (principally retail financing), earnings are accounted for over the terms of the receivables on the sum-of-the-digits (Rule of 78ths) basis. With respect to notes receivable in which the face amount represents the principal (principally wholesale and interest-bearing lease financing), the interest is taken into income as accrued; unpaid interest accrued at the balance sheet date is included in accounts receivable.

Financing Losses and Loss Provisions: Loss allowances are maintained in amounts considered by management to be appropriate in relation to receivables outstanding at the respective statement dates. Losses sustained are charged either directly to income or, in the case of certain types of losses (principally on non-recourse retail receivables and on foreign receivables), to the related allowance account.

Losses arising from repossession of the collateral supporting doubtful accounts are charged off as soon as disposition of the collateral has been effected and the amount of the deficiency has been determined. Where repossession has not been effected, losses are charged off as soon as it is determined that the collateral cannot be repossessed, generally not more than 150 days after default.

Insurance Operations: Insurance premiums are taken into income on a basis related to coverage provided over the terms of the policies (principally pro rata). Commission costs and premium taxes incurred in acquiring new business are deferred and amortized over the terms of the related policies on the same basis as premiums are earned. The liability for unpaid losses and claims includes a provision for unreported losses based on past experience. The estimated salvage and subrogation recoverable on both paid and unpaid losses is recognized at the time the losses are recorded.

2. CASH

The Company is required to maintain compensating balances against lines of credit under agreements with banks in the United States (see Note 4). Such funds are maintained in demand deposit accounts and are not subject to withdrawal restrictions. These compensating balances are generally equivalent over a period of time to 10% of the credit lines and, in the case of certain of such credit lines, an additional 10% of any borrowings thereunder. Compensating balances maintained by the Company averaged $351.8 million for the year 1977 and $309.3 million for 1976. In Canada and other countries, compensating balances are not required.

Figure 1.8   Part 5

3. FINANCE RECEIVABLES

The distribution of maturities of finance receivables outstanding at December 31, 1977 and December 31, 1976 is summarized as follows:

	United States	Canada	Other Countries	Total
			(In thousands of dollars)	
December 31, 1977				
Retail and Lease Financing Receivables (a)				
Due in 1978	$ 6,746,068	$ 480,892	$ 619,838	$ 7,846,798
Due in 1979	4,510,951	295,556	358,482	5,164,989
Due after 1979	2,597,372	123,285	190,300	2,910,957
Total	13,854,391	899,733	1,168,620	15,922,744
Wholesale Receivables (principally due on demand)...........................	6,920,834	670,354	548,861	8,140,049
Term Loans to Dealers	73,456	10,597	15,473	99,526
Accounts Receivable	105,045	9,650	13,951	128,646
Total	$20,953,726	$1,590,334	$1,746,905	$24,290,965
December 31, 1976				
Retail and Lease Financing Receivables (a)				
Due in 1977	$ 5,727,929	$ 496,030	$ 514,283	$ 6,738,242
Due in 1978	3,820,078	308,027	303,218	4,431,323
Due after 1978	1,900,381	125,368	153,469	2,179,218
Total	11,448,388	929,425	970,970	13,348,783
Wholesale Receivables (principally due on demand)...........................	5,449,995	610,963	508,250	6,569,208
Term Loans to Dealers	74,713	10,549	15,156	100,418
Accounts Receivable	81,178	9,043	8,544	98,765
Total	$17,054,274	$1,559,980	$1,502,920	$20,117,174

(a) Includes Leasing Receivables.

Average earning finance receivables outstanding on a consolidated basis were $19,610.0 million in 1977 and $16,162.9 million in 1976.

Figure 1.8 Part 6

19

3. FINANCE RECEIVABLES (concluded)

Past due instalments and repossession balances due at December 31, 1977 and December 31, 1976 on retail and lease financing receivables outstanding, which are included with the amounts due within one year in the foregoing tabulation, are as follows:

	United States	Canada	Other Countries	Total
	(In thousands of dollars)			
December 31, 1977				
Past due instalments excluding reposses-sions				
Past due 30 days or less	$136,380	$14,873	$9,689	$160,942
Past due over 30 days	18,264	1,038	1,345	20,647
Repossessions (balances due)	61,839	3,659	2,420	67,918
December 31, 1976				
Past due instalments excluding reposses-sions				
Past due 30 days or less	119,444	13,934	7,540	140,918
Past due over 30 days	16,553	1,226	823	18,582
Repossessions (balances due)	53,194	4,749	1,899	59,842

Wholesale receivables and term loans to dealers past due over 30 days aggregated $10.5 million at December 31, 1977 and $5.2 million at December 31, 1976.

Losses on all finance receivables amounted to $56.6 million in 1977 and $49.5 million in 1976.

4. NOTES, LOANS AND DEBENTURES PAYABLE WITHIN ONE YEAR

	December 31,	
	1977	1976
	(In thousands of dollars)	
Short-term notes		
Commercial paper—United States	$ 5,954,006	$4,973,206
Unamortized discount	(10,023)	(47,763)
Net amount..	5,943,983	4,925,443
Other—United States	2,143,590	1,619,872
Canada	584,224	443,883
Other countries	340,063	321,815
Total principal amount	3,067,877	2,385,570
Unamortized discount	(10,636)	(11,339)
Net amount	3,057,241	2,374,231
Bank loans and overdrafts		
United States...	10,000	—
Canada	17,461	7,238
Other countries..	579,420	505,020
Total..	606,881	512,258
Other notes, loans and debentures payable within one year		
United States		
Medium-term notes	346,125	248,029
Other	175,000	235,000*
Canada	261,604	229,195
Other countries..	89,108	81,106
Total principal amount	871,837	793,330
Unamortized premium	43	17
Net amount	871,880	793,347
Total notes, loans and debentures payable within one year	$10,479,985	$8,605,279

*Includes senior subordinated indebtedness of $5.0 million payable within one year.

Figure 1.8 Part 7

4. NOTES, LOANS AND DEBENTURES PAYABLE WITHIN ONE YEAR (concluded)

In the United States, commercial paper is issued in varying terms ranging up to 270 days; other short-term notes represent borrowings on a demand basis arranged under agreements with trust departments of certain account banks. Bank loans are made on both a demand and time basis.

Unused lines of credit from banks were $4,222.7 million at December 31, 1977 and $3,742.2 million at December 31, 1976. Such unused lines of credit were available for short-term borrowings.

In the United States, the average interest rates for each category of short-term borrowings, based on the dollar amount outstanding at December 31, 1977 and December 31, 1976, were as follows:

	December 31,	
	1977	1976
	%	%
Commercial paper	6.50	5.13
Other short-term notes	6.85	4.63
Bank loans	4.75	—

In Canada and other countries, interest rates on short-term borrowings ranged up to 8¼% and 23%, respectively, at December 31, 1977 and to 9¼% and 21%, respectively, at December 31, 1976.

On a consolidated basis, the maximum amount of short-term borrowings outstanding at any month end was $9,629.0 million during 1977 and $7,871.0 million during 1976. The average amount of such borrowings outstanding was $8,231.0 million during 1977 and $7,130.0 million during 1976. The weighted average interest rates thereon were 6.04% in 1977 and 6.05% in 1976. These rates have been determined by relating the short-term interest costs for the period to the daily average dollar amounts outstanding.

5. ACCOUNTS PAYABLE TO DEALERS

These accounts represent credits to dealers withheld by GMAC. At the time of purchase of retail instalment contracts supported by a dealer guaranty, GMAC retains out of the proceeds due the dealer and credits the dealer with a percentage (generally 1% for each year of the contract term in the case of new cars and 2% in the case of used cars) of the amount identified in the instalment contracts as the unpaid balance upon which the dealer computes his finance charge to the instalment buyer. GMAC holds such portion of these amounts credited to the dealer as it considers sufficient for its protection in the event of the dealer's inability or failure to discharge his obligation to GMAC.

With respect to the contracts supported by a guaranty, the dealer is responsible to GMAC in accordance with the Retail Plan for payment of the unpaid balance of the retail obligation, except in cases where GMAC is unable to retake the car from a retail buyer in default and turn it over to the dealer within a specified period of time. In order, however, to provide automotive dealers with an opportunity to limit their responsibility for future repossessions, GMAC has included in the GMAC Retail Plan an Optional Non-Recourse Plan, which is available at the request of the dealer. Under its provisions a dealer may, at his option, limit his losses on repossessions to the dealer credits held by GMAC. Such credits must, at the time the option is exercised, be equal to an agreed percentage, generally 3% (the minimum percentage) but in any event not more than 6%, of the aggregate unpaid balance under the retail contracts purchased from the dealer and then outstanding. Of the total accounts payable to dealers, $10.2 million at December 31, 1977 and $10.4 million at December 31, 1976 represent credits applicable to dealers who have exercised the option under the Optional Non-Recourse Plan.

Figure 1.8 Part 8

21

0553811

GENERAL MOTORS ACCEPTANCE CORPORATION
AND SUBSIDIARIES

NOTES TO
FINANCIAL STATEMENTS
(continued)

6. NOTES, LOANS, DEBENTURES AND SUBORDINATED INDEBTEDNESS WITH TERMS OF MORE THAN ONE YEAR FROM DATES OF ISSUE

The aggregate principal amounts of notes, loans, debentures and subordinated indebtedness, with terms of more than one year from dates of issue, maturing in each of the five years following December 31, 1977 and December 31, 1976 are as follows:

	December 31, 1977	December 31, 1976
	(In thousands of dollars)	
First year (included in Note 4)	$860,363	$780,437
Second year	696,098	573,397
Third year	772,371	401,893
Fourth year	580,343	488,012
Fifth year	332,944	394,496

7. ADDITIONAL DEBT

In February 1978, the Company issued $150.0 million of 8.20% notes due February 15, 1988 and $150.0 million of 8.65% debentures due February 15, 2008.

8. STOCKHOLDER'S EQUITY

The Company increased its authorized and outstanding $100 par value common stock by the issuance and sale at par to General Motors Corporation of 1,000,000 shares in June 1976 and 1,500,000 shares in June 1977. In January 1978, the Company further increased its authorized and outstanding $100 par value common stock by the issuance and sale at par to General Motors Corporation of 2,000,000 additional shares.

The agreements with respect to outstanding subordinated indebtedness include, among other things, provisions which have the effect of limiting the payment of dividends by the Company. Under the most restrictive of these provisions, approximately $575.7 million at December 31, 1977 of net income retained for use in the business was available for the payment of dividends.

Figure 1.8 Part 9

9. SEGMENT INFORMATION

Industry segments: The business of the Company and its subsidiaries is comprised of financing and insurance operations.

Gross revenue, income before income taxes and assets applicable to financing and insurance operations are as follows:

	1977	1976
	(In thousands of dollars)	
Gross revenue		
Financing operations	$ 1,976,785	$ 1,670,941
Insurance operations	384,289	269,198
Eliminations(a)	(25,263)	(17,885)
Total	$ 2,335,811	$ 1,922,254
Income (loss) before income taxes		
Financing operations	$ 375,010	$ 334,147
Insurance operations	35,652	(2,633)
Total	$ 410,662	$ 331,514
Assets at end of period		
Financing operations	$23,137,027	$19,067,961
Insurance operations	503,652	367,365
Eliminations(b)	(6)	(3,142)
Total	$23,640,673	$19,432,184

(a) Intersegment insurance premiums earned.

(b) Intersegment insurance receivables and, in 1976, a reclassification of insurance income tax benefits receivable.

Figure 1.8 Part 10

9. SEGMENT INFORMATION (concluded)

Geographic segments: Although much the greater part of its business is done in the United States, the Company also operates directly or through subsidiaries in Canada and many other countries around the world.

Gross revenue, income before income taxes and assets applicable to the United States, Canada and other countries are as follows:

	1977	1976
	(In thousands of dollars)	
Gross revenue		
United States	$ 1,986,959	$ 1,594,493
Canada	153,637	156,261
Other countries	195,215	171,500
Total	$ 2,335,811	$ 1,922,254
Income before income taxes		
United States	$ 355,767	$ 285,292
Canada	13,988	17,916
Other countries	40,907	28,306
Total	$ 410,662	$ 331,514
Assets at end of period		
United States	$20,517,547	$16,573,074
Canada	1,528,522	1,487,432
Other countries	1,594,604	1,371,678
Total	$23,640,673	$19,432,184

10. SUPPLEMENTARY INCOME STATEMENT INFORMATION

The following items have been charged to operating expenses:

	1977	1976
	(In thousands of dollars)	
Taxes other than income taxes	$37,425	$31,667
Rents	22,172	18,844
Depreciation	8,607	7,596

The Company and its subsidiaries currently provide for depreciation of company automobiles in the United States at the rate of 2½% per month, in Canada on a declining balance method at the rate of 30% per annum, and in other countries generally at the rate of 2% per month. In the United States, depreciation of office equipment is generally calculated on the sum-of-the-years digits method, and in other countries on the local income tax basis.

At the time office equipment or company automobiles are retired or otherwise disposed of, the difference between the net book amount and the proceeds of sale or salvage is generally reflected in income as a charge or credit against the provision for depreciation.

Figure 1.8 Part 11

24

106064

11. UNITED STATES, FOREIGN AND OTHER INCOME TAXES

	1977	1976
	(In thousands of dollars)	
Income taxes estimated to be payable currently		
United States Federal...	$150,375	$122,060
Foreign	26,785	21,567
United States state and local	19,655	20,475
Total payable currently	196,815	164,102
Deferred income taxes—net	8,475	6,173
Total income tax expense	$205,290	$170,275

Deferred income taxes represent the tax effects of timing differences between pretax accounting income and taxable income principally related to provisions for losses on finance receivables and to policy acquisition expense.

The Company and its domestic subsidiaries join with General Motors Corporation in filing a consolidated United States income tax return. The portion of the consolidated tax recorded by the Company and its domestic finance subsidiaries is equivalent to the amount which would be required if the Company and such subsidiaries filed a separate consolidated tax return; the portion recorded by the insurance subsidiary is equivalent to its contribution to the consolidated tax liability.

The provision for income taxes as a percentage of pretax accounting income differs from the statutory rate for Federal income taxes (48%) principally because of the provision for state and local income taxes and the non-taxability of certain dividend and interest income.

12. PENSION PROGRAM

The Company and its subsidiaries participate in various pension plans of General Motors Corporation and its domestic and foreign subsidiaries, which cover substantially all of their employes. The total expense allocated to the Company and its subsidiaries, amounting to $27.0 million in 1977 and $20.4 million in 1976, is determined on the basis of actuarial cost methods and includes amortization of prior service cost over periods not exceeding 30 years. With the exception of certain overseas subsidiaries, pension costs accrued are funded.

The actuarially computed value of vested benefits of all plans in which the Company and its subsidiaries participate exceeded the total of pension funds, at market, and balance sheet accruals as of December 31, 1977, by approximately $760 million. This amount represents the unfunded portion of the actuarially computed present value of pension benefits to which employes are entitled based on service as of December 31, 1977, and is calculated as if all employes were to terminate service as of that date. This figure is in excess of the estimated liability for benefits guaranteed under the Employee Retirement Income Security Act in the event of plan termination.

Under the actuarial cost method employed by General Motors Corporation, approximately $2.1 billion of the prior service costs applicable to all plans in which the Company and its subsidiaries participate had not been funded or otherwise provided for at December 31, 1977. These prior service costs generally result from periodic amendments which have been made to the pension plans, and are being amortized and funded over periods not exceeding 30 years. While the portion of unfunded vested pension benefits and unfunded prior service costs which relates to employes of the Company and its subsidiaries is not determinable, the number of such employes represents less than 9% of the total number of employes covered by the plans.

Figure 1.8   Part 12

25

13. TRANSACTIONS WITH AFFILIATES

The amount due General Motors Corporation and affiliated companies at the balance sheet dates relates primarily to current wholesale financing of sales of General Motors products consisting of in-transit items and amounts on which settlement to General Motors for automotive wholesale financing is deferred beyond transit time.

Leasing receivables at December 31, 1977 and December 31, 1976 include approximately $23 million and $15 million, respectively, resulting from the lease of computers and related equipment to various units of General Motors.

Insurance premiums earned in 1977 and 1976 include $73.1 million and $20.9 million, respectively, earned by Motors Insurance Corporation, commencing September 1, 1976, as a co-insurer with a non-affiliated company of certain product and other liability coverages provided to General Motors. Motors Insurance Corporation also provides certain insurance coverages to GMAC; earned premiums thereon, amounting to $25.3 million in 1977 and $17.9 million in 1976, have been eliminated in the consolidated financial statements.

14. CONTINGENT LIABILITIES

There are various claims and pending actions against the Company and its subsidiaries in respect of taxes and other matters arising out of the conduct of the business. Certain of these actions purport to be class actions. The amounts of liability on these claims and actions at December 31, 1977 were not determinable but, in the opinion of the management, the ultimate liability resulting will not materially affect the consolidated financial position or results of operations of the Company and its subsidiaries.

15. MARKETABLE SECURITIES

At December 31, 1977, the difference between market value and cost of stocks consisted of gross unrealized profits (excess of market value over cost) of $51.8 million and gross unrealized losses (excess of cost over market value) of $4.2 million. During January 1978, net unrealized losses, before income taxes, on stocks were approximately $7.2 million.

16. UNAUDITED SUMMARY OF CONSOLIDATED INCOME BY QUARTER

An unaudited summary of consolidated income by quarter for the Company and its subsidiaries for the years 1977 and 1976 is as follows:

	Gross Revenue	Interest and Discount	Operating Expenses	Financing Losses and Loss Provisions	Insurance Losses and Loss Expense	Income Taxes	Net Income
			(In thousands of dollars)				
1977-First Quarter ...	$ 539,282	$ 253,558	$114,112	$15,991	$ 61,537	$ 46,610	$ 47,474
-Second Quarter .	573,207	275,255	120,343	14,698	60,343	50,310	52,258
-Third Quarter ..	599,758	293,730	114,476	17,049	64,028	56,317	54,158
-Fourth Quarter .	623,564	306,877	116,167	21,667	75,318	52,053	51,482
Total	$2,335,811	$1,129,420	$465,098	$69,405	$261,226	$205,290	$205,372
1976-First Quarter ...	$ 445,242	$ 210,955	$ 93,695	$14,700	$ 43,678	$ 42,173	$ 40,041
-Second Quarter.	471,059	225,331	99,721	17,665	45,338	41,788	41,216
-Third Quarter..	489,327	236,526	101,561	16,891	47,523	44,533	42,293
-Fourth Quarter .	516,626	240,889	112,305	19,376	64,586	41,781	37,689
Total	$1,922,254	$ 913,701	$407,282	$68,632	$201,125	$170,275	$161,239

Figure 1.8   Part 13

1.7 MANAGEMENT RESPONSIBILITY FOR CASH FLOW

In this chapter we have simply tried to get cash flow in perspective, in particular to demonstrate how and why it flows and how it differs from profits. But cash flow does not flow of its own accord—it can only do so as a direct consequence of management decisions. . . taken either consciously and positively or unconsciously by default. Subsequent chapters will deal with forecasting and control of cash flow by management, so perhaps it would be useful to summarize this chapter with a list identifying those major management decision areas which *cause* cash to flow—for good or ill. Much of what has been discussed in this chapter can be distilled into the following ten decision areas which determine cash flows for a firm and set up the differences between profit and cash flow:

1 *Operating decisions*—the same range of decisions which contribute to profit before charging depreciation: earlier in this chapter we referred to this amount as cash flow from operations, but to be more correct we should call it *potential* cash flow from operations because the following further decision areas will add to or subtract from this amount in practice.

2 *Capital expenditure decisions*—the acquisition or disposal of plant, equipment, or such other assets of a long lasting nature which result in a depreciation charge against profits.

3 *Inventory decisions*—changes in the amounts tied up in stocks of raw materials, finished goods, work-in-progress, sub-assemblies, service spares, etc.—increases in inventory create a negative cash flow; decreases effectively create a positive cash flow in that cash outflow on replenishment of inventory is avoided.

4 *Customer credit decisions*—the length of time the customers are permitted to take before paying for sales invoiced to them (note that profit on sales is normally computed as soon as the invoice is raised)—an increase in customer credit delays cash inflow, reduction of credit accelerates it.

5 *Supplier credit policies*—the length of time we take before we pay for materials, services and other items invoiced to us—an increase in supplier credit effectively creates a positive cash flow in that it delays cash outflow; reduction of credit accelerates cash outflow.

6 *Other accepted credit terms [an extension of (5)]* —e.g. rent, telephone, electricity and certain taxes (such as VAT or value added tax settlement in the UK), that is where it is normal to pay or receive at periodic intervals in advance or

in arrears. The accounting process will tend to "smooth out" the charge against profits.

7 *Tax on profits [an extension of (6)]* —tax on corporate profits is due and payable at certain dates predetermined by law and consequently has a significant impact upon the pattern of cash outflows. (For example, in the UK an advance payment—ACT or advance corporation tax—is made when and if a dividend is paid but the balance is payable in one amount on one date which for a particular company might be fixed between nine and twenty-one months after the end of the financial year in which the profits arose.)

8 *Financial obligations*—interest and dividend payments plus any contractual repayments of capital arising from past financial decisions.

The impact of the above groups will determine the net cash surplus or deficit at any point in time which clearly leads to a final pair of groups:

9 *Investing decisions*—the utilization of surplus funds by the purchase of investment or, conversely, the liberation of funds by sale of such investment.

10 *Financing decisions*—the acquisition of new money either from shareholders or by borrowing on a short- or long-term basis from outside the firm (including the use of installment purchasing, hire purchase, or leasing to finance capital expenditure decisions).

In subsequent chapters, we shall examine in greater depth the significance of and inter-relationship of these management decision areas in the context of cash planning, forecasting, and control.

Wenman Plastics:
Part 1

Karl Wenman was born in Switzerland in 1910 and came to England in the early 1950s with considerable experience in precision engineering, toolmaking and moldmaking. He set himself up in business and gradually developed an expertise in the supply of molds and molding equipment to the developing plastics industry. The onset of financial difficulties at one of his major customers led to a merger with that customer which brought Karl Wenman into the plastics industry itself. Wenman Plastics Limited was incorporated on April 1, 1962.

Through the 1960s Wenman Plastics steadily grew and gained an established place in the plastics industry, earning for itself a high reputation for quality plastic products, primarily in the domestic container market but also as subcontractor to certain national manufacturers of domestic appliances and toys. By 1970, Karl Wenman was chairman and managing director of Wenman Plastics and was also a substantial shareholder: the balance of shares was held by close relatives, friends and business acquaintances. However, in 1970, Karl Wenman was sixty and felt that the time was coming nearer for his son Claude to join the firm—an event for which both father and son had long planned.

Claude had taken an engineering degree in Switzerland and a masters degree in business administration at one of the European business schools. He later joined one of the major European chemical companies and with their plastic packaging subsidiary gained experience in development, production, and marketing in both England and Germany. In 1970, Claude was thirty-five years old.

Claude was appointed joint managing director of Wenman Plastics Ltd on January 1, 1972 and immediately put into operation his ideas for the development of the company. During his earlier experiences, he had observed certain opportunities in the market for plastic products which had not been considered appropriate for his previous employer. Further development and market research during 1972 confirmed that the following two product ranges were worthy of exploitation.

1 A range of modular bathroom accessories produced in a high-quality, heavy-duty, scratch-resistant, and shatter-proof plastic material: initially the range would consist of eight items with a choice of five colors to be sold through hardware stores: the range was capable of further expansion as the market developed.

2 The design and provision of heavy-duty special-purpose plastic packaging to a wide range of industrial suppliers for whom more traditional packing materials were becoming increasingly scarce or expensive or where the product itself had previously not been packaged: individual contracts would be negotiated with interested firms.

A number of prospective customers expressed considerable interest in the early prototypes and promised trial orders. Claude was convinced that a broad-scale introduction was the only way to make a significant impact on the market. So he pursued his research and the following picture began to emerge (please note that all amounts are expressed to the nearest $1000).

1 Existing Financial Position

An estimated balance sheet for Wenman Plastics on March 31, 1973 is reproduced in summary form as Exhibit 1.

2 Market Potential

a Claude estimated that sales of Wenman Plastics could very quickly be doubled to $6000 per annum, although to allow for establishment and running in, a figure of $5250 ought to be projected for the first year's operation to March 31, 1974.

b Sales of the new products ought to begin in a small way in June 1973, building up to their full potential by August 1973.

	$ '000s	$ '000s
Fixed Assets		
Land and buildings	500	
Plant, equipment and vehicles	300	
		800
Net Current Assets		
Inventory:		
Raw material	300	
Work-in-progress	100	
Finished goods	100	
	500	
Sundry debtors (accounts receivable)	648	
Short-term investments	100	
Bank balances and cash	10	
	1258	
Deduct:		
Sundry creditors (accounts payable)	(108)	
Current tax (due January 1, 1974)	(150)	
Unpaid dividend	(50)	
		·950
		$1750
Ordinary shares of $1 each		500
Accumulated undistributed profits		1250
		$1750

Exhibit 1 Wenman Plastics: estimated balance sheet as of March 31, 1973 (summary only to the nearest $1000)

3 Facilities

a Existing premises were inadequate to house both existing and new production, but fortunately Claude was able to rent additional premises with all necessary services provided and within easy reach of the existing factory. Occupation would be possible on April 1, 1973.

b If the factory began to operate on a two-shift basis, additional plant equipment, and vehicles (including initial alterations to the new premises and also normal plant replacements for the year to March 31, 1974) were estimated to cost $1000.

4 Production Policy

a Sales in the past had only ever been mildly seasonal (low sales typical in August and February being offset by high sales in October and March) and, therefore, a policy of producing at a steady level had always been followed. Inventory levels and annual holiday shutdown provided the necessary buffer. Claude saw no reason to change this policy but there would clearly be some delay in working up to capacity once the new equipment was installed.

b Recruitment and training of additional staff was progressing, and Claude expected that the new factory could begin production during April and would be fully operational during May in anticipation of the build up of sales referred to above.

5 Inventory Policy

Claude felt that the following levels would provide adequate safeguards against failure in delivery of raw materials, imbalance in production, and inability to meet sales demand from stock:

1 Raw materials: two months normal production requirement.

2 Work-in-progress: two weeks normal production.

3 Finished goods: two months average sales demand.

6 Income and Expenditure

A complete reorganization of production would be necessary and therefore past experience was only a general guide. However, Exhibit 2 reproduces Claude's estimated profit statement for Wenman Plastics for the year ending March 31, 1973 and his projection for the year to March 1974 based upon detailed cost estimates, and budgets, and the comments made above.

Exhibit 2 Wenman Plastics: estimated profit statement (summary only to nearest $1000)

Year to March 31, 1973			Year to March 31, 1974	
$'000s	$'000s		$'000s	$'000s
3000		Sales		5250
		Less direct cost of sales:		
	900	Materials	1733	
1700	800	Labor	1312	3045
1300		Gross margin		2205
	280	Salaries and related expenses	480	
	300	Rent, rates, electricity, and telephone	400	
		Other running expenses:		
	150	Production	250	
	100	Administration	120	
	30	Advertising	80	
900	40	Selling and distribution	80	1410
		Potential cash flow from		
400		operations		795
100		*Deduct:* Depreciation charge		300
$300		Profit before interest and tax		$495

7. Financing

Claude realized that the following factors needed to be taken into his further calculations:

a It was customary in the trade both to take and offer monthly credit terms (for example, purchases in April would not be paid for until early June).

b Karl Wenman was reluctant to issue any new ordinary shares in the company as this would dilute the family control.

c Furthermore, Karl insisted that the present 20% dividend on ordinary share capital should be maintained.

d Short-term investments had been built up to help finance the new products and appear in Exhibit 1 at their realizable value.

e The existing premises were freehold, had a current value somewhat in excess of their balance sheet value, and Claude had received an intimation from a finance house in London that it would be possible to obtain a loan of up to $450, on security of the property, carrying interest at 16%.

At this stage, Claude pondered the financial viability of the operation and therefore sat down to project a balance sheet as of March 31, 1974. He realized that this document would reflect the financial position one year hence and would therefore show whether the company would need to raise more funds than were immediately available through the processes indicated above.

Question 1

Claude has produced a forecast profit statement and will shortly produce a forecast balance sheet. This latter document will reveal any need for additional cash as of March 31, 1974.

Identify and set down the conscious decisions that either Karl or Claude have made which will have a critical impact upon the requirements for cash—quite apart from the impact upon profits. Explain why and how the decisions you set down have their impact upon the requirement for cash and how this requirement might differ if the decision were changed.

Question 2

Produce the forecast balance sheet that Claude is about to produce. How much, if any, additional cash will be required to carry the operation of March 31, 1974?

Measuring and Forecasting Cash Flow

Having gotten clear in our minds the nature of cash flow
and the range of management decisions
that determine both the quantities and timing of cash flow
it is but a short and logical step
to attempt to predict cash flows
and to take such steps as are necessary to control them.
If a firm is to continue in existence, its management
should at least plan to keep away from bankruptcy!
So in this chapter we turn to the principles
of analyzing cash movements
as a basis for their measurement,
control, forecasting, and reporting.

2.1 FRAMEWORK FOR ANALYSIS

In the preceding chapter we looked in some depth at the determinants both of the quantities and of the timing of cash flow, and we have underlined management's responsibility for exercising control over cash flow. If management is to fulfill this responsibility, it would seem sensible that financial information be made available in the appropriate form and at the appropriate time to guide management decisions. The form, or framework, for compiling such financial information is by no means unimportant because it will serve the triple functions of:

1 Providing information on cash movements *historically*.

2 Monitoring *current* cash movements to indicate potential areas for management control action.

3 Forecasting *future* cash movements.

35

An appropriate framework, therefore, deserves some careful study if it is to form the triple basis for management's diagnosis, control, and planning.

What will be an appropriate framework for presenting information on cash flow (as is the case with the presentation of any piece of financial information) depends to a great extent on the information that management requires in order to guide its decision making. The information requirements of management depend in turn upon the key elements over which management is able to exercise   control. Therefore, in determining a framework for analysis we must ask ourselves what are those key elements in the movement of cash flow that management must control. Clearly, different firms may have different critical factors that must be monitored and controlled and the framework for presenting information on cash flow must therefore be specifically tailored to the needs of each individual firm. Section 1.6 in the preceding chapter, which dealt with the significance of the industrial environment, indicated some of the factors that might be critical in individual circumstances. However, Section 1.7 listed ten representative management decision areas that help to shape the movement of cash flow in any firm. We therefore have a fairly sound base from which to discuss at least the principles of designing an appropriate framework for analysis.

Broadly speaking there are two methods of approach. Each will produce the same answer but they are looked at from different points of view. The two methods and their application will be described in greater detail shortly, but in summary they are:

1 *The cash book method*—which is designed to measure cash flow on the basis of the classified entries which appear in the cash book. The cash book is a commonly used basic book of account that records how much cash is collected from customers, how much is paid to suppliers, how much is paid in wages and so on. The logic of the cash book *method* is that it relates to the way in which the bookkeeping system records actual cash inflows and outflows and therefore provides a ready basis for comparison.

2 *The cash tank method*—which is designed to measure cash flow not by an accounts classification but by the areas of management responsibility that gave rise to the decisions which originally determined cash flows (for example, the ten decision areas which formed the basis of Section 1.7). The logic of this method is that it relates to the areas of management responsibility that form the basis for management control action.

The two methods are not in conflict—they simply have different orientations. In fact, both might find application within a firm simultaneously as we shall see. Before discussing applications, however, let us first spend a little time in examining the mechanics of each method.

2.2   THE CASH BOOK METHOD OF ANALYSIS

When a firm receives or pays out cash or checks in the daily conduct of its business affairs, each receipt or payment is for a specific purpose, e.g. collections from customers, payments for wages, rent and telephone. The purpose for which each item is received or paid forms the basis for the accounts classification which, when summarized via the bookkeeping process, provides the routine accounting reports that culminate in the profit statement and balance sheet. The basic bookkeeping record is the cash book: in this is entered each item of receipt and payment by cash or checks, in chronological sequence, indicating its appropriate accounts classification. A fairly obvious basis of analyzing cash movements is thus simply to summarize the entries in the cash book. There could, of course, be many headings of accounts classification, but for our purpose we are not overly concerned with detail; rather we are concerned with rough cuts which indicate only the major groups of receipt and payment. Furthermore, it is useful if the analysis also indicates the degree to which management is able to exercise control over any item of cash flow as to either its amount or timing. On this basis a relatively short list of headings of receipts and payments will present itself.

2.2.1   Receipts

1   From customers, i.e. collections of accounts receivable or debtors.

2   From cash sales not involving credit.

3   From miscellaneous repetitive sources, e.g. rents, interest, dividends and royalties.

4   From miscellaneous non-repetitive sources, e.g. disinvestments (sale of surplus assets or investments) and new sources of finance (bank borrowings, loans, new issues of shares).

2.2.2   Payments

5   To suppliers of raw materials and other supplies, i.e. reduction of accounts payable or creditors.

6   To employees for weekly wages and monthly salaries and also including any

Line No.		APL	MAY	JUN	JUL	AUG	SEP	OCT	NOV	DEC	JAN	FEB	MAR
	CASH RECEIPTS												
1	Collections from customers												
2	Cash sales												
	Miscellaneous:												
3	Routine, e.g. rent, interest												
4	Special, e.g. sale of assets												
5	TOTAL RECEIPTS (R)												
	CASH PAYMENTS												
6	Payments to suppliers												
7	Wages, salaries and labor-related exps												
8	Miscellaneous routine items												
9	Rent, telephone, electricity, rates												
10	Taxes												
11	Purchase of buildings, plant, equipment												
12	Interest and dividend payments												
13	Repayment of borrowings												
14	Special items												
15	TOTAL PAYMENTS (P)												
17	CURRENT SURPLUS (DEFICIT): (R − P)												
18	Cash and bank balances at end of previous month												
19	CASH AND BANK BALANCES AT END OF CURRENT MONTH												

Figure 2.1 Analysis of cash movements using the cash book method

necessary labor related expenses, e.g. national or local insurance or pension contributions and income tax deductions from employee remuneration.

7 For miscellaneous repetitive purposes not incorporated either above or below: the amount here will be relatively insignificant in amount and is unlikely to vary greatly from one month to the next.

8 To public utilities and other providers of services where settlement is on a regular basis, perhaps quarterly, half yearly or yearly, e.g. rent, telephone, electricity and rates (property taxes).

9 For the settlement of other tax liabilities, e.g. tax on corporate profits and, for example, in the UK, value added tax.

10 For capital expenditures, e.g. the acquisition of land, buildings, plant and equipment: representing significant, discrete but irregular payments.

11 To meet financial obligations: those of a regular nature, e.g. interest or dividend payments; and those of an irregular nature, e.g. repayment of loans.

12 For any other purpose of a significant, irregular or extraordinary nature, e.g. settlement of litigation.

The above list is representative, not exhaustive: other items may represent matters of greater consequence to an individual firm. However the list does represent, under significant groupings, the major sources of cash inflow and outflow; moreover, as the list of payments moves down from (5) to (12) it moves more into those areas for maneuver where management decisions in the short term can have a significant impact upon the pattern of cash flow: for example, there is little that management can do *in the short term* to change the rate of cash outflow on wages and salaries, but there is more that can be done to dictate the amount and/or timing of payments for capital expenditures.

Using the above framework, an analysis of cash flows on a monthly basis could take the form shown in Figure 2.1.

2.3 THE CASH TANK METHOD OF ANALYSIS

If a firm runs out of cash it would at worst be forced out of business or at least be forced to accept considerable constraints upon its freedom of action. It is for this reason that management must take appropriate steps to ensure that the firm does not run out of cash. In this context, let us think of cash as the vital contents of a tank which must not be allowed to run dry. We can extend the analogy to any tank containing a valuable liquid which must not be allowed to run dry: if such a tank is fitted with inlet pipes and outlet pipes, each provided with a control valve, it is clear that the level of liquid in the tank can only be controlled by one of two courses of action:

1 Reducing or eliminating outflows by adjusting the valves on one or more of the outlet pipes.

2 Increasing inflows by adjusting the valves on one or more of the inlet pipes.

A schematic diagram of such a liquid flow system appears in Figure 2.2, showing the main tank, feeder tanks, inlet pipes and outlet pipes with the control valves (marked by rectangular blocks). Note that the control valve regulates both the rate and timing of flow.

Against the background of this physical model of liquid flow it is but a short step to visualize a cash flow system that adopts the same concepts. The main elements of such a system are incorporated into the schematic diagram shown in Figure 2.3. Only three feeder tanks have been shown, representing the three major groups of source of cash inflow: operations, new money, and liquidation of assets. Similarly, each main group of inflows has its counterpart group of outflows: appropriations of profit on taxes and dividends; servicing or repayment of borrowings; acquisition of assets. If management is to control the level of cash in the tank, these are the three main groups of inflow and outflow that must be tackled.

The cash tank analysis brings into focus those areas of management responsibility where decisions were made which caused cash to flow. This is the

Figure 2.2 Schematic diagram of liquid flow system

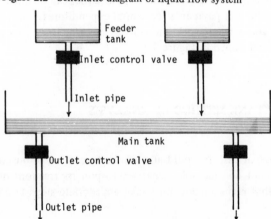

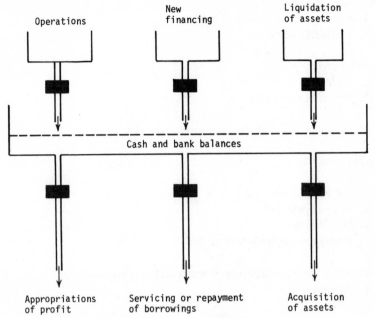

Figure 2.3 Schematic diagram of main elements of cash flow system

main point of difference from the cash book method of analysis which concentrated, via accounts classification, upon the source of inflows and the destination of outflows. Pursuing the tank analogy to its conclusion, the cash tank method, therefore, concentrates upon the valves that must be controlled by management in order to preserve the level of cash in the tank. Adjustment of the valves controls the rate or timing of the flow of cash in from the feeder tanks via the inlet pipes (representing sources of cash inflows), or down through the outlet pipes (representing cash outflows). The valves will, in fact, represent the ten management decision areas that were summarized in Section 1.7 as the major determinants of cash flow. These ten decision areas are repeated here in abbreviated form for convenience:

1 Operating decisions—culminating in potential cash flow from operations before tax.

2 Capital expenditure decisions:
    a. Acquisition (purchase)
    b. Disposal (sale)

3 Inventory decisions:
    a. Increases in inventory
    b. Decreases in inventory

4 Customer credit decisions:
   a. Increase or extension of credit
   b. Reduction of credit

5 Supplier credit policies:
   a. Increase or extension of credit
   b. Reduction of credit

6 Other accepted credit terms—very similar to (5)

7 Taxes on profits

8 Financial obligations:
   a. Interest payment
   b. Dividend payment
   c. Repayment of borrowed capital

9 Investing decisions—utilization of temporary surplus funds:
   a. Purchase
   b. Sale

10 Financing decisions—acquisition of new money:
   a. From shareholders
   b. By borrowing

Our cash tank can now be completed and appears in Figure 2.4. Further feeder tanks and outlet pipes have been added and the control valves have been numbered to coincide with the ten management decision areas summarized above. Different inlet and outlet pipes in practice have different bore diameters, allowing a lot or a little to pass through at the turn of a valve. Some inlet valves can be left open for a long time (hopefully number 1, for example) while others have a limited reserve in the feeder tank (5a, for example). Some valves can be activated frequently, others less frequently. Some outlet valves must be opened periodically whether management wishes it or not (7, for example). The art of cash management is knowing which valves to turn on or off . . . and when.

     The analogy of a cash tank which we have just described can form a useful framework of analysis for an alternative approach to the measurement of cash flow. Such a summary, prepared on a monthly basis could take the form shown in Figure 2.5. The sequence of entries follows that developed in our cash tank in Figure 2.4 reading from left to right across the tank both for inflows and outflows. This method should be compared with the cash book method of analysis demonstrated in Figure 2.1. The final three lines (numbered 17, 18, and 19) under each method must of course give the same numbers: only the approach is

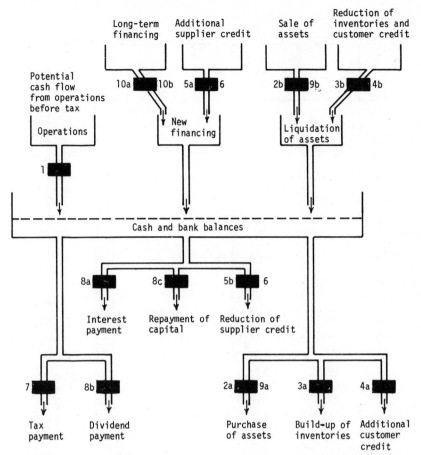

Figure 2.4 Schematic diagram of the cash tank method for analyzing cash movements—the numbers against the control valves correspond to the ten management decision areas summarized in the text

different. This can be verified by reference to the two examples prepared as cash forecasts for Wenman Plastics and reproduced in Exhibits 5 and 6 found in Chapter 3.

2.4 FORECASTING CASH MOVEMENTS

Thus far in this chapter we have concentrated our attention primarily on the two methods of measuring cash flow in a historic context. It is now time to turn our

Line No.		APL	MAY	JUN	JUL	AUG	SEP	OCT	NOV	DEC	JAN	FEB	MAR
	INFLOWS OF CASH												
1	Operations before tax												
	New sources of capital:												
2	Long-term financing												
3	Additional supplier credit												
	Liquidation of surplus assets:												
4	Sale of fixed assets												
	Reduction of current assets:												
5	Decrease in inventories												
6	Reduction of customer credit												
7	TOTAL INFLOWS (I)												
	OUTFLOWS OF CASH												
8	Tax payment												
9	Dividend payment												
10	Interest payment												
11	Repayment of capital												
12	Reduction of supplier credit												
	Acquisition of assets:												
13	Purchase of fixed assets												
	Build-up of current assets:												
14	Increase in inventories												
15	Additional customer credit												
16	TOTAL OUTFLOWS (O)												
17	CURRENT SURPLUS (DEFICIT): (I − O)												
18	Cash and bank balances at end of previous month												
19	CASH AND BANK BALANCES AT END OF CURRENT MONTH												

Figure 2.5 Analysis of cash movements using the cash tank method

attention to the principles of forecasting cash flow. We shall see that the principles of, and in particular the two methods of measuring, cash flow historically have equal application in the forecasting context. Because cash flow is so critical to a firm, surely it is essential that management attempt to forecast the likely pattern of future cash flows if only as a minimum precaution against business failure. Such a forecast will doubtlessly not prove to be precisely accurate, but nevertheless it will still yield sufficiently reliable signposts to indicate where, when, and what (if any) type of action needs to be taken by management if the firm is to avoid financial catastrophe or is to seize financial opportunity. This, of course, is true of any forecast: a "good" forecast is not necessarily the one that turns out to be "right" but the one which, as the future unfolds, provides the basis for guiding appropriate and timely management action.

It will not be possible to compile a cash forecast without expending both time and effort, and this leads one to question whether it is all worthwhile. One can only judge by considering the benefits that accrue to the firm from the expenditure of this time and effort. The following are the benefits that should accrue from a systematic approach to cash forecasting:

1 *Avoidance of bankruptcy*—Clearly this is the ultimate aim of any business and this alone should justify the cash forecast.

2 *Avoiding costly mistakes*—Short of bankruptcy, many firms suffer the financial consequences of ill-considered or hastily undertaken ventures. A cash forecast will reveal in advance the potential impact on cash flow of such a venture. By revealing the possible consequences in advance there should still be time to reconsider the venture or its timing: it is too late to be wise after the event!

3 *Assisting management control*—The cash forecast will provide early warning of an impending cash problem and indicate steps that management might take to reduce or eliminate its impact.

4 *Increased confidence by the lender*—It becomes less difficult to raise funds when required if management can demonstrate that it is attempting to be in command of the situation by predicting if, when, for how long, and in what amounts additional funds will be required. It could be too late to attempt to raise funds *after* the onset of financial difficulties.

5 *Improved utilization of capital*—Not only is it the function of a cash forecast to indicate cash deficiencies or requirements for finance; it will also indicate if cash surpluses are likely to arise. In these circumstances, management can take appropriate measures to utilize the cash surplus to maximum advantage.

In the preceding chapter we stressed the importance of the timing of cash flow. The time dimension must be restressed at this stage because it must never be overlooked that when compiling a cash forecast, one is not only attempting to forecast quantities but also the *timing* of cash flows. Even though all the quantities of future cash flows have been forecast correctly, the firm could still find itself in considerable financial difficulty if the forecast of the time were seriously wrong; suppose for example, that all the cash inflows, though forecast correctly in amount, in fact came one month later than planned, while all the outflows, though forecast correctly in amount, in fact went out one month earlier than planned. The example in Figure 2.6 demonstrates this significance in timing. Notice that the forecast and actual quantities of both inflow and outflow are identical and therefore the actual cash position in total remains exactly as planned. However, the actual cash inflows have come one month later than planned while the actual outflows have gone out one month earlier than planned. The forecast showed a favorable cumulative cash position throughout the six months, whereas the actual was considerably and continuously negative until the end.

Hopefully by now we have justified the need for a cash forecast but in fact this need is twofold. A firm needs to be aware of its potential future cash flows not only in the short term but also in the longer term. Therefore, there are, broadly speaking, two types of cash forecast:

1 The short-term forecast.

2 The long-term forecast.

The two types have slightly different objectives and orientations and therefore will be dealt with separately in this book. A brief description of each now follows.

Figure 2.6   Demonstration of significance of timing of cash flows

CASH FORECAST (SIMPLIFIED)							
	JAN	FEB	MAR	APL	MAY	JUN	TOTAL
Forecast inflows	100	200	300	200	200	–	1000
Forecast outflows	–	80	160	240	160	160	800
Monthly cash surplus (deficit)	100	120	140	(40)	40	(160)	
Cumulative cash surplus (deficit)	100	220	360	320	360	200	200

ACTUAL CASH FLOWS FOR THE SITUATION FORECAST ABOVE							
	JAN	FEB	MAR	APL	MAY	JUN	TOTAL
Actual inflows	–	100	200	300	200	200	1000
Actual outflows	80	160	240	160	160	–	800
Monthly cash surplus (deficit)	(80)	(60)	(40)	140	40	200	
Cumulative cash surplus (deficit)	(80)	(140)	(180)	(40)	nil	200	200

2.5 SHORT-TERM CASH FORECASTS

The prime objective of a short-term cash forecast is to ensure that a firm can pay its debts in the immediate future: it is thus oriented towards the guidance of appropriate management control action in the short term. For this reason, it needs to be up-to-date and reasonably detailed; hence it will be prepared at frequent intervals and will cover the upcoming six to twelve months. Either of the two methods of analysis described in this chapter will provide a suitable framework for the forecast but the cash book method (see Section 2.2 and Figure 2.1) tends to be more frequently used because:

1 It highlights the actual detailed cash receipts and cash payments that management will seek to control.

2 It forms a more ready basis of comparison with the analysis of actual cash flows from the cash book.

3 Some of the data required for the cash tank method of analysis may not readily be available on a monthly basis.

The subject of short-term cash forecasting will form the basis for Chapter 3.

2.6 LONGER-TERM CASH FORECASTS

The object of preparing a cash forecast over the longer term is to indicate the financial consequences of future strategic courses of action and to assist in long-term financial planning. This objective is quite different from that of a short-term forecast so it is not surprising to find a different approach and format in use. The long-term cash forecast will be prepared perhaps only annually; it will tend to cover the upcoming five years and will be in much more global terms; its orientation will be towards the financial consequences of and inter-relationship between strategic management decisions. It is clear that the cash tank method of analysis (see Section 2.3 and Figure 2.5) will provide a much more useful framework under these circumstances. The cash book method is too concerned with detail to provide a valuable framework for the long-term forecast. The subject of long-term cash forecasting will form the basis for Chapter 5.

2.7   REPORTING CASH MOVEMENTS

Before returning to the mechanics of cash forecasting (an internal problem for the firm) it might be of value to digress briefly into a related area and to review the current state of the art of reporting cash movements to interested parties outside the firm.

Shareholders (or stockholders) and bondholders are protected by law in most countries and such protection will require the minimum provision of financial information. For example, in the United Kingdom, the Companies Acts provide legal safeguards for the shareholder of a limited company (or corporation), and these provisions include a requirement for the publication of an audited balance sheet and profit statement at least once in every calendar year, with supplementary information supplied half yearly. Other countries have their own similar legal requirements and, over and above domestic legislation, each country has to some degree take account of the pressures of public opinion, trade unions and similarly organized labor pressure groups, the organized stock exchange and professional accounting bodies. These pressures are stronger in some countries than in others. The definition of "interested party" to whom financial information shall be reported and the form that such information takes differ, then, from country to country; they also differ over time within the same country.

We have seen that cash flow is vital to a firm's existence and indeed is much more important than profit in the short term. Therefore, when reporting financial information to shareholders and other interested parties, should cash flow be made a feature of such a report? Clearly, it would be of value to the shareholders because such information can reveal much more about performance and prospects than an analysis of the profit statement (or income statement) and balance sheet alone. Only a few countries, however, have a legal or professional requirement for the reporting of such information (e.g. the U.S.A., Canada, Peru, and South Africa). The document which must be produced, in addition to the Balance Sheet and Profit Statement, is variously entitled; the most common terms are "Statement of Change in Financial Position", "Statement of Source and Application of Funds", or "Funds Flow Statement". Strictly speaking, "cash flow" and "funds flow" are not synonymous terms. "Cash flow" deals solely with the inflow and outflow of cash, while "funds flow" deals with all the elements that make up the flow of working capital. Working capital is broader in coverage than cash; it includes not only cash, but all current assets, from which all current liabilities are deducted. For all practical purposes, however, in the context of this book, "cash flow" and "funds flow" will be treated as synonymous.

The recipient of published information is clearly interested in the quality of management performance. For this reason, if a statement of cash movements is published, the cash tank method of analysis is recommended for this purpose, although the actual format might not best be displayed in the manner demonstrated in Figure 2.5. An alternative structure will be suggested in Chapter 5 and we shall return briefly to this discussion at that time. Figures 2.7–2.17 are examples.

Where does the quest for improved reporting end? Who are "interested parties" and to what extent should a company lay bare its innermost secrets? Does reporting end with historical information or should it incorporate forecasts? If so, how long should it be before a company must publicly report its cash forecast? These are questions upon which the reader is invited to ponder while reviewing the "march of progress" in information reporting technology and practice.

American Broadcasting Companies, Inc. and Subsidiaries

Statements of Changes in Consolidated Financial Position

	1977	1976
Working capital provided from:		
Operations:		
Net earnings	$109,795,000	$ 71,747,000
Add expenses not requiring working capital:		
Depreciation and amortization of property and		
equipment	18,138,000	16,602,000
Provision for long-term deferred income tax	(5,498,000)	5,202,000
Amortization of intangibles	2,970,000	1,502,000
Writedown of assets of the Wildlife Preserve	—	3,500,000
Other	1,454,000	1,052,000
Working capital provided from operations	126,859,000	99,605,000
Increase in long-term debt	18,000,000	499,000
Increase in deferred income	4,529,000	1,694,000
Exercise of employee stock options	7,735,000	4,102,000
Disposal of property and equipment	1,998,000	2,045,000
Sale of investments	—	102,000
Other	4,502,000	(1,567,000)
	163,623,000	106,480,000
Working capital used for:		
Purchase of property and equipment	46,262,000	28,565,000
Acquired intangibles	21,477,000	164,000
Payment of cash dividends	19,544,000	14,804,000
Reduction of long-term debt	7,097,000	7,052,000
Increase in television program rights, non-current	17,903,000	—
Funds restricted for additions to property and equipment	14,382,000	—
	126,665,000	50,585,000
Increase in working capital	$ 36,958,000	$ 55,895,000
Changes in Components of Working Capital:		
Increase (decrease) in current assets:		
Cash and marketable securities	$ 15,308,000	$ 85,491,000
Receivables, less allowances	36,392,000	30,355,000
Television program rights, production costs		
and advances, less amortization	(6,688,000)	10,471,000
Inventory of merchandise and supplies	(8,915,000)	6,465,000
Prepaid expenses	5,379,000	7,916,000
	41,476,000	140,698,000
Increase (decrease) in current liabilities:		
Accounts payable and accrued expenses	16,989,000	36,168,000
Federal income taxes	(12,488,000)	48,588,000
Long-term debt payable within one year	17,000	47,000
	4,518,000	84,803,000
Increase in working capital	$ 36,958,000	$ 55,895,000

Figure 2.7

AMERICAN TELEPHONE AND TELEGRAPH COMPANY
AND ITS CONSOLIDATED SUBSIDIARIES

STATEMENTS OF CHANGES IN FINANCIAL POSITION

	Thousands of Dollars				
	1977	1976	1975	1974	1973
SOURCE OF FUNDS:					
From Operations:					
Income before Extraordinary Item	$ 4,543,933	$ 3,829,151	$ 3,147,722	$ 3,174,464	$ 2,951,147
Add—Expenses not requiring funds:					
Depreciation	5,045,312	4,483,906	4,088,089	3,690,390	3,332,403
Deferred income taxes	1,686,374	1,488,938	1,403,841	1,263,239	867,384
Investment tax credits—net	731,619	705,054	667,322	258,263	225,209
Deduct—Income not providing funds:					
Interest charged construction	228,619	216,284	239,957	240,902	223,283
Share of equity-basis companies' income in excess of dividends	110,731	58,806	—	99,031	119,264
Total funds from operations	11,667,888	10,231,959	9,067,017	8,046,423	7,033,596
Proceeds from sale of investment in "Comsat"	—	—	—	—	104,484
From Financing:					
Issuance of shares	1,597,196	1,212,637	1,022,651	223,637	1,058,985
Issuance of long and intermediate term debt	2,285,000	2,026,500	2,545,000	2,956,000	2,809,000
Total funds from financing	3,882,196	3,239,137	3,567,651	3,179,637	3,867,985
Increase in ownership interest of others in certain consolidated subsidiaries	360,979	35,298	35,960	24,698	78,418
Decrease (increase) in working capital	743,050	204,521	(994,726)	1,069,609	(66,013)
	$16,654,113	$13,710,915	$11,675,902	$12,320,367	$11,018,470
APPLICATION OF FUNDS:					
Telephone plant	$11,292,729	$ 9,747,710	$ 9,354,661	$ 9,816,812	$ 9,077,277
Dividends	2,822,163	2,488,875	2,166,360	2,039,800	1,782,912
Increase in deferred charges	182,351	173,174	145,805	72,933	107,251
Reduction of long and intermediate term debt	2,310,129	1,295,000	110,000	180,000	60,000
Change in investments at cost	15,517	24,106	(13,310)	24,691	12,338
Acquisition of part of the ownership interests of others in consolidated subsidiaries	—	—	—	11,942	—
Change in investments in companies accounted for on an equity basis	11,217	25,325	(8,300)	139,725	10,406
Other—net	20,007	(43,275)	(79,314)	34,464	(31,714)
	$16,654,113	$13,710,915	$11,675,902	$12,320,367	$11,018,470
The decrease (increase) in working capital is accounted for by:					
Increase in current liabilities:					
Accounts payable	$ 225,776	$ 286,396	$ 22,774	$ 157,648	$ 97,107
Taxes accrued	10,638	288,591	13,617	(121,603)	348,369
Advance billing and customers' deposits	84,561	70,131	72,725	49,062	52,789
Dividends payable	94,918	81,238	19,361	52,795	54,169
Interest accrued	9,047	35,042	65,421	66,860	50,611
Debt maturing within one year—Note (7)	777,561	242,381	(721,342)	1,161,835	(398,030)
	1,202,501	1,003,779	(527,444)	1,366,597	205,015
Less—Increase in current assets:					
Cash and temporary cash investments, net of drafts	(203,654)	363,190	1,922	61,608	(65,312)
Receivables	550,775	379,841	405,931	143,889	289,081
Material and supplies	119,813	93,138	612	80,711	31,130
Prepaid expenses	(7,483)	(36,911)	58,817	10,780	16,129
	459,451	799,258	467,282	296,988	271,028
Decrease (increase) in working capital, as above	$ 743,050	$ 204,521	$ (994,726)	$ 1,069,609	$ (66,013)

See Notes to Financial Statements.

Figure 2.8

CBS Inc. and Subsidiaries

CONSOLIDATED STATEMENTS of
CHANGES in FINANCIAL POSITION

———

	Years Ended December 31	
	1977	1976
	(Dollars in Thousands)	
Sources of working capital:		
Income from operations	$182,008	$163,995
Items not affecting working capital:		
Depreciation and amortization	40,679	33,417
Deferred income taxes	(7,911)	7,537
Income from investments accounted for under the equity method	(7,438)	(4,154)
Working capital provided by operations	207,338	200,795
Issuance of treasury shares under employee benefit plans	6,401	8,124
Increase in amounts due after one year, other than long-term debt	6,169	1,645
Decrease in investments	590	2,345
Other, net	3,521	3,390
Total sources	224,019	216,299
Uses of working capital:		
Cash dividends	58,873	50,275
Purchase of property, plant and equipment	63,932	46,042
Purchase of treasury shares	66,247	20,606
Decrease (increase) in long-term debt	(284)	2,263
Increase in intangible and other assets	54,359	4,050
Total uses	243,127	123,236
Net increase (decrease) in working capital	$(19,108)	$ 93,063

Figure 2.9

Consolidated Statement of Changes in Financial Position

Chrysler Corporation and Consolidated Subsidiaries
(in millions of dollars)

	Year ended December 31	
Additions to working capital:	1977	1976
From operations:		
Earnings before extraordinary item	$ 124.8	$ 328.2
Depreciation	165.4	140.8
Amortization of special tools	222.6	261.3
Changes in deferred income taxes—noncurrent	(9.9)	32.6
Equity in net earnings of unconsolidated subsidiaries	(36.3)	(20.8)
Loss (gain) on translation of long-term debt	18.5	(22.8)
	485.1	719.3
Extraordinary item	38.4	94.4
Proceeds from long-term borrowing	279.0	87.3
Proceeds from sale of common stock	.4	1.6
Retirement of property, plant and equipment	5.0	49.0
Increase in other liabilities	24.8	8.0
Increase in minority interest	.4	3.1
Decrease (increase) in investments and advances	47.9	(65.9)
Other	11.8	13.7
TOTAL ADDITIONS	892.8	910.5
Dispositions of working capital:		
Cash dividends paid	54.3	18.1
Expenditures for property, plant and equipment	386.3	227.4
Expenditures for special tools	336.8	196.7
Reduction in long-term borrowing	104.9	70.3
TOTAL DISPOSITIONS	882.3	512.5
INCREASE IN WORKING CAPITAL DURING THE YEAR	$ 10.5	$ 398.0

	Increase (Decrease) in Working Capital	
Changes in components of working capital:		
Cash and marketable securities	$(163.2)	$ 344.3
Accounts and notes receivable	99.1	113.0
Current and deferred taxes on income	60.5	(54.9)
Inventories	268.6	285.2
Accounts payable and accrued expenses	(193.7)	(480.9)
Short-term debt	(77.5)	201.9
Other	16.7	(10.6)
	$ 10.5	$ 398.0

Pension Plans
Current service costs of pension plans are accrued and funded on a current basis. Prior service costs are amortized and funded over periods not exceeding thirty years.

Other Retirement Benefits
The cost of continuing life insurance provided upon retirement is accrued in a manner similar to pension costs, but is not funded. Health insurance cost for retirees is charged to income as applicable premiums are paid.

Cost of Investments in Consolidated Subsidiaries in Excess of Equity
To the extent that the cost of the investments in majority-owned and controlled subsidiaries exceeds the equity in net assets of the subsidiaries at dates of acquisition, such differences, if incurred after October 31, 1970, are amortized over periods not exceeding twenty years. Such amounts incurred prior to October 31, 1970 are not amortized.

Investment Tax Credit
Reductions in taxes resulting from the investment credit provisions of the United States Internal Revenue Code are being taken into income at the time the related assets are placed in service.

Inventories
Inventories are stated at the lower of cost or market, with cost determined substantially on a first-in, first-out basis.

Product Warranty
Estimated lifetime costs of product warranty are accrued at the time of sale.

Figure 2.10

53

THE DOW CHEMICAL COMPANY AND SUBSIDIARIES
STATEMENT OF CHANGES IN FINANCIAL POSITION
For the Five Years Ended December 31, 1977
(Thousands of Dollars)

	1973	1974	1975	1976	1977
SOURCE OF WORKING CAPITAL:					
Net income before extraordinary items and cumulative effect of change in accounting	$271,148	$ 563,874	$ 632,385	$ 612,767	$ 555,703
Charges (credits) to income not involving working capital:					
Depreciation (Note O)	263,114	327,235	347,428	404,181	478,625
Equity in net income of non-consolidated companies, less dividends received	(33,168)	(62,928)	(40,344)	(40,561)	(69,217)
Deferred income taxes	36,927	134,806	80,033	64,107	37,722
Other — net	7,473	3,953	1,824	1,203	772
Proceeds from sale of investments, less gains reflected in net income	5,921	19,039	4,543	4,764	3,208
Provided from operations	551,415	985,979	1,025,869	1,046,461	1,006,813
Extraordinary items		10,969			
Issuance of long-term debentures and notes	93,300	29,869	225,000	320,000	528,425
Issuance of pollution control bonds		29,834	97,525		
Pollution control funds released by trustees				31,036	27,636
Increase in other long-term debt	37,046	8,944			
Sale of common stock to employees	22,763	26,616	37,659	46,994	7,268
Increase in other liabilities	8,987	38,522	6,753		
Decrease in deferred charges	1,093				
Decrease in noncurrent investments					39,638
Disposal of plant property and sundry	12,140	26,215	20,904	15,153	38,772
	726,744	1,156,948	1,413,710	1,459,644	1,648,552
USE OF WORKING CAPITAL:					
New property, plant and equipment	401,663	870,048	921,471	1,186,193	1,163,016
Cash dividends declared	89,868	111,074	138,974	176,181	211,674
Purchase of treasury stock	8,614	35,360	38,790	67,659	97,318
Decrease in long-term debt			64,520	4,728	40,298
Increase in unexpended pollution control funds		20,584	77,955		
Increase in noncurrent investments	50,745	32,491	6,106	23,983	
Increase in deferred charges and other		17,066	3,346	22,031	9,230
Acquisition of subsidiaries and purchase of minority interests	4,749	10,699			
	555,639	1,097,322	1,251,162	1,480,775	1,521,536
INCREASE (DECREASE) IN WORKING CAPITAL	$171,105	$ 59,626	$ 162,548	$ (21,131)	$ 127,016
INCREASE (DECREASE) IN CURRENT ASSETS:					
Cash and marketable securities	$155,162	$ 105,661	$ (48,432)	$ (242,665)	$ 3,108
Receivables	139,488	248,899	25,630	258,853	100,482
Deferred taxes	9,877	45,412	5,949	(6,229)	6,668
Inventories	73,673	225,102	91,944	184,303	68,643
DECREASE (INCREASE) IN CURRENT LIABILITIES:					
Notes payable and current portion of long-term debt	54,300	(15,399)	(76,891)	(148,527)	(76,796)
Accounts payable	(135,840)	(227,224)	37,502	(126,760)	26,506
Income taxes and accruals	(125,555)	(322,825)	126,846	59,894	(1,595)
INCREASE (DECREASE) IN WORKING CAPITAL	$171,105	$ 59,626	$ 162,548	$ (21,131)	$ 127,016

Figure 2.11

ELI LILLY AND COMPANY AND SUBSIDIARIES

CONSOLIDATED STATEMENTS OF CHANGES IN FINANCIAL POSITION

	Year Ended December 31	
	1977	1976 Restated (Note B)
SOURCE OF WORKING CAPITAL		
Net income	$218,684,000	$202,682,000
Charges to income not involving working capital:		
Depreciation—Schedule VI	41,355,000	35,930,000
Amortization of intangible assets	384,000	384,000
Deferred taxes	18,017,000	8,312,000
TOTAL FROM OPERATIONS	278,440,000	247,308,000
Proceeds from sales of common stock under option plans	240,000	363,000
Issuance of common stock in satisfaction of performance awards	526,000	–
Disposals of property and equipment—Schedules V and VI	7,721,000	3,676,000
Additions to long-term debt	–	12,926,000
Decrease in other assets	3,488,000	–
Other credits to additional paid-in capital	–	57,000
	290,415,000	264,330,000
USE OF WORKING CAPITAL		
Cash dividends	98,991,000	86,900,000
Additions to property and equipment—Schedule V	78,157,000	68,531,000
Increase in other assets	–	6,058,000
Reductions of long-term debt	19,635,000	4,744,000
	196,783,000	166,233,000
INCREASE IN WORKING CAPITAL	$ 93,632,000	$ 98,097,000
CHANGES IN COMPONENTS OF WORKING CAPITAL		
Increases (decreases) in current assets:		
Cash and securities	$ 39,901,000	$ 65,456,000
Receivables	23,076,000	21,209,000
Inventories	69,542,000	25,232,000
Prepaid expenses	(759,000)	3,203,000
	131,760,000	115,100,000
Increases (decreases) in current liabilities:		
Loans payable	45,020,000	(29,414,000)
Accounts payable	(967,000)	11,648,000
Employee compensation and payroll taxes	9,775,000	4,487,000
Other liabilities	(4,423,000)	10,690,000
Federal and foreign income taxes	(11,277,000)	19,592,000
	38,128,000	17,003,000
INCREASE IN WORKING CAPITAL	$ 93,632,000	$ 98,097,000

Figure 2.12

CONSOLIDATED STATEMENT OF CHANGES IN FINANCIAL POSITION

	Year Ended	
	January 1, 1978	January 2, 1977
	(In thousands)	
Financial resources were provided by:		
Operations:		
Net income	**$11,162**	$12,456
Charges (credits) to income not affecting working capital:		
Depreciation and amortization	**18,309**	16,663
Deferred income taxes	**2,111**	917
Provision for employee benefits	**1,645**	307
Other	**(686)**	(481)
Financial resources provided by operations	**32,541**	29,862
Increase in common stock and additional paid-in capital	**386**	3,089
Proceeds from disposition of property, plant and equipment	**2,067**	1,399
Proceeds from long-term borrowings	**7,863**	22,699
Total financial resources provided	**42,857**	57,049
Financial resources were applied to:		
Expenditures for property, plant and equipment	**22,047**	36,076
Cash dividends	**4,292**	4,265
Reduction of long-term debt	**3,465**	3,193
Long-term investments	**5,842**	–
Other	**(111)**	156
Total financial resources applied	**35,535**	43,690
Increase in working capital	**$ 7,322**	$13,359
Changes in elements of working capital:		
Current assets – increase (decrease):		
Cash and temporary cash investments	**$16,143**	$ 1,704
Accounts and notes receivable	**(9,560)**	25,585
Inventories	**(18,528)**	3,505
Accumulated income tax prepayments	**1,195**	(3,987)
Prepaid expenses and other current assets	**2,208**	1,863
	(8,542)	28,670
Current liabilities – (increase) decrease:		
Notes payable to banks	**4,806**	(4,163)
Current installments of long-term debt	**128**	(712)
Accounts payable	**1,888**	(5,163)
Accruals – compensation, employee benefits and other	**736**	(3,036)
Estimated income taxes payable	**8,306**	(2,237)
	15,864	(15,311)
Increase in working capital	**$ 7,322**	$13,359

Figure 2.13

56

INTERNATIONAL BUSINESS MACHINES CORPORATION
AND SUBSIDIARY COMPANIES

CONSOLIDATED STATEMENT OF CHANGES IN FINANCIAL POSITION
For the year ended December 31:

	1977	1976
	(Thousands of Dollars)	
Source of working capital:		
Net earnings	$2,719,414	$2,398,093
Depreciation and other items not requiring the current use of working capital	2,553,852	2,237,970
Total from operations	5,273,266	4,636,063
Proceeds from stock sold under employee plans	305,698	293,862
Long-term borrowings	22,701	24,800
	5,601,665	4,954,725
Application of working capital:		
Investment in plant, rental machines and other property	3,394,741	2,518,234
Less: Depreciation of manufacturing facilities capitalized in rental machines	193,353	141,115
	3,201,388	2,377,119
Increase in deferred charges and other assets	176,351	88,083
Cash dividends paid or payable	1,910,747	1,203,791
Reduction of long-term debt	42,052	44,788
Treasury stock purchased for employee plan	340,641	154,648
Capital stock purchased and canceled	904,538	—
	6,575,717	3,868,429
Increase (decrease) in working capital	$ (974,052)	$1,086,296
Changes in working capital:		
Cash and marketable securities	$ (749,632)	$1,387,946
Notes and accounts receivable	478,364	325,851
Inventories and prepaid expenses	423,618	91,780
U.S. Federal and non-U.S. income taxes	(82,529)	(298,980)
Accounts payable and accruals	(564,224)	(518,689)
Loans payable	(56,529)	98,388
Dividend payable	(423,120)	—
Increase (decrease) in working capital	(974,052)	1,086,296
Working capital at beginning of year	5,838,125	4,751,829
Working capital at end of year	$4,864,073	$5,838,125

Figure 2.14

MONSANTO COMPANY AND SUBSIDIARIES

STATEMENT OF CHANGES IN CONSOLIDATED FINANCIAL POSITION
FOR THE FIVE YEARS ENDED DECEMBER 31, 1977

	Year				
	1977	1976	1975	1974	1973
			(Dollars in millions)		
Source of Working Capital:					
Net income	$ 275.6	$ 366.3	$306.3	$323.2	$238.3
Charges not affecting working capital:					
Depreciation, obsolescence and depletion	296.0	226.0	172.7	171.9	170.3
Deferred income taxes	54.7	61.5	66.1	23.7	2.8
Other — net	28.4	14.3	6.7	(14.5)	(8.1)
Working capital from operations	654.7	668.1	551.8	504.3	403.3
Outside financing — net of unexpended funds from industrial development bonds	126.3	81.7	296.0	8.0	6.6
Property disposals	26.9	20.3	12.2	18.6	15.9
Proceeds from issuance of capital stock	2.0	8.8	5.8	16.9	19.2
	809.9	778.9	865.8	547.8	445.0
Application of Working Capital:					
Property, plant and equipment additions	607.1	646.8	527.7	313.4	205.3
Dividends	111.4	100.9	93.1	83.9	69.3
Debt reduction	79.0	33.6	31.6	18.7	20.1
Other — net	38.3	41.3	31.6	18.5	(26.9)
	835.8	822.6	684.0	434.5	267.8
Increase (Decrease) in Working Capital	$ (25.9)	$ (43.7)	$181.8	$113.3	$177.2
Changes in Elements of Working Capital:					
Increase (decrease) in current assets:					
Cash, time deposits and short-term securities	$(121.9)	$(105.4)	$101.5	$(66.2)	$195.6
Net receivables	79.6	51.7	158.6	35.5	85.1
Inventories	94.6	105.7	(110.7)	242.7	(0.2)
	52.3	52.0	149.4	212.0	280.5
(Increase) decrease in current liabilities:					
Accounts payable and accruals	(34.2)	(89.9)	(19.1)	(101.5)	(44.0)
Income taxes	(15.8)	(1.8)	58.5	2.4	(57.2)
Current portion of long-term debt	(28.2)	(4.0)	(7.0)	0.4	(2.1)
	(78.2)	(95.7)	32.4	(98.7)	(103.3)
Increase (Decrease) in Working Capital	$ (25.9)	$ (43.7)	$181.8	$113.3	$177.2

Figure 2.15

58

Polaroid Corporation and Subsidiary Companies
Consolidated Statement of Changes in Financial Position
Years ended December 31, 1977 and 1976 (In thousands)

Source and use of funds	*1977*	*1976*
Source of funds		
Net earnings	$ 92,284	$ 79,690
Items not requiring current outlay of funds:		
Depreciation of property, plant and equipment	39,524	38,271
Loss on disposal of property, plant and equipment	773	420
Funds derived from operations	132,581	118,381
Proceeds from sale of property, plant and equipment	758	361
Total source of funds	133,339	118,742
Use of funds		
Additions to property, plant and equipment	68,759	33,890
Cash dividends	21,356	13,470
Total use of funds	90,115	47,360
Increase in working capital	$ 43,224	$ 71,382

Changes in components of working capital		
Current assets—Increase (decrease)		
Cash	$ 37,927	$ 31,553
Marketable securities	(83,777)	47,346
Receivables	91,748	22,532
Inventories	38,489	11,272
Prepaid expenses	5,519	7,760
Total change in current assets	89,906	120,463
Current liabilities—(Increase) decrease		
Notes payable to banks	(19,267)	(18,720)
Payables and accruals	(39,045)	(20,403)
Federal, state and foreign income taxes	11,630	(9,958)
Total change in current liabilities	(46,682)	(49,081)
Increase in working capital	$ 43,224	$ 71,382

Figure 2.16

RCA CORPORATION AND SUBSIDIARIES

CONSOLIDATED STATEMENT OF CHANGES IN FINANCIAL POSITION

	Year Ended December 31,	
	1977	1976
	(in millions)	
Sources of funds		
Net profit for the year	$ 247.0	$ 177.4
Other charges (credits) not requiring outlay of funds		
Depreciation, including revenue-earning equipment of Hertz: 1977, $164,800,000; 1976, $145,200,000	332.0	300.2
Reduction in value of the investment in United Kingdom food companies	—	20.0
Deferred tax expense	63.0	54.4
Interest during construction capitalized by communications companies	(8.0)	(13.0)
Total from operations	634.0	539.0
Decrease (increase) in inventories	5.0	(15.9)
Dispositions of plant and equipment	41.5	45.2
Increase in accounts payable and accruals	182.6	43.6
Proceeds from issuance of debt of RCA Alascom	90.0	—
Increase in debt of Hertz	81.6	21.2
Other	9.3	11.5
	1,044.0	644.6
Uses of funds		
Cash dividends paid on preferred and common stock	91.1	79.9
Increase in accounts receivable	130.9	13.3
Increase in prepaid expenses, excluding deferred taxes	105.2	5.2
Additions to revenue-earning equipment of Hertz (less net value of vehicles replaced: 1977, $318,700,000; 1976, $284,800,000)	280.0	219.9
Increase in other assets	36.2	41.4
Additions to plant and equipment, excluding interest during construction capitalized by communications companies	262.5	262.4
Decrease in notes payable, excluding current portion of long-term debt	16.4	102.0
Decrease (increase) in taxes on income	4.0	(9.5)
Payments of other long-term debt	32.4	31.6
	958.7	746.2
Increase (decrease) in funds	85.3	(101.6)
Cash and equivalents—beginning of year	178.2	279.8
Cash and equivalents—end of year	$ 263.5	$ 178.2

Figure 2.17

60

Wenman Plastics:
Part 2

Please note that all amounts are expressed to the nearest $1000. Readers are first invited to review Part I of this case study and to compare their own forecast balance sheet (produced in response to Question 2) with that which appears as Exhibit 3.

Claude Wenman looked at his forecast balance sheet for Wenman Plastics as of March 31, 1974 (reproduced as Exhibit 3). It revealed a cash deficit of $684 as of that date. He realized that this was the additional finance that his company must raise if the decisions that had been made regarding expansion of the company were to be put into effect—and if all his estimates turned out correctly.

He was a little perturbed by the size of this deficit and was curious to first analyze exactly how it had arisen despite both an estimated operating profit for 1973/74 and the availability of a substantial secured loan.

	$'000s	$'000s
Fixed Assets		
Land and buildings	500	
Plant, equipment and vehicles[1]	1,000	1,500
Net Current Assets		
Inventory[2]		
Raw material	330	
Work-in-progress	145	
Finished goods	580	
	1,055	
Sundry debtors (accounts receivable)[4]	1,080	
Short-term investments	-	
Bank balances and cash	-	
	2,135	
Deduct		
Sundry creditors (accounts payable)[4]	(378)	
Current taxation (due January 1,1975)	(200)	
Unpaid dividend	(50)	1,507
		3,007
Ordinary shares of $1 each	500	
Accumulated undistributed profits[3]	1,373	
TOTAL SHAREHOLDERS' CAPITAL EMPLOYED	1,873	
Secured loan on security of property	450	2,323
DEFICIT: Additional requirement for finance		$684

Exhibit 3 Wenman Plastics Forecast Balance Sheet as of March 31, 1974

Nevertheless he felt that even if he did require the full $684 it would be possible to obtain this on reasonably favorable terms from a bank or other financial institution because:

1 There was ample coverage in plant and equipment, inventories and sundry debtors (accounts receivable) to provide security.

2 There would be a good cash flow from future operations to provide for repayment if Exhibit 2 were a reliable guide.

But one further thought troubled him. He realized that the timing of cash flow was an important feature in any forecast and could be of considerable importance in this operation due to the need to establish new production facilities and new markets. Therefore, before seeking banking assistance for his future cash requirements he determined to perform one further piece of analysis which

```
Notes (amounts in $'000s)

1  Plant, equipment and vehicles calculated as follows:

   Amount at March 31,1973 as per Exhibit 1        300
   Additional investment                         1,000
                                                 ─────
                                                 1,300
   Deduct depreciation charge per Exhibit 2        300
                                                 ─────
   Balance as at March 31,1974                   1,000
                                                 ═════

2  Inventory levels are all calculated on the basis of average
   monthly sales of $500 (at rate of $6,000 p.a.) and using
   direct cost of sales relationships from Exhibit 2, viz.

   Materials       33% or $165 per month
   Labor           25% or $125 per month

3  Accumulated undistributed profits calculated as follows:

   Trading profit before interest and tax (Exhibit 2)   495
   Deduct Interest - $450 at 16%                          72
                                                        ─────
   Profit before tax                                    423
   Deduct Estimated tax, say                            200
                                                        ─────
   Profit after tax                                     223
   Deduct Dividend at 20%                               100
                                                        ─────
   Undistributed profit: added to retentions            123

   Undistributed profits at March 31,1973 (Exhibit 1) 1,250

   Accumulated undistributed profits at March 31,1974 1,373
                                                      ══════

4  Sundry debtors includes $80 addition for VAT (value added
   tax) and similarly sundry creditors includes $28.
```

Exhibit 3, continued

would reveal the cash inflows and outflows on a monthly basis throughout the year ending March 31, 1974. In this way he hoped to ascertain whether the amount of $684 at the end of March in fact represented the amount of peak requirement for further financing. He therefore looked again at the estimates which he had made (and which were summarized in Part I) and tried to assess the incidence of the various items of income and expenditure throughout the year. Exhibit 4 summarizes his opinions in this respect.

Question 3

Claude first wished to show how the deficit of $684 had arisen. The "cash tank" method of analysis will reveal this. Produce such an analysis (in total only—not month by month) for the year ended on March 31, 1974.

	TOTAL	Apl	May	Jun	Jul	Aug	Sep	Oct	Nov	Dec	Jan	Feb	Mar
Sales invoiced[1]	5250	250	250	350	400	200	500	800	500	500	500	200	800
Purchases[2]	2060	110	200	200	250	50	150	200	200	150	200	200	150
Labor[3]	1540	78	153	136	136	102	102	170	136	102	170	136	119
Salaries and related expenses[4]	480	38	38	38	38	38	42	42	42	42	42	42	42
Rent, rates, electricity and telephone	400	110			80			75			135		
Other running expenses[5]	530	30	44	27	30	93	62	30	32	66	33	33	50
Additional plant, equipment and vehicles	1000	400	400			100					100		
Ordinary dividend	100	50						50					
Interest on secured loan	72			18			18			18			18

Notes

1 No price increase anticipated during the year. Spread of sales allows early establishment of new production facilities followed by normal mildly seasonal pattern.

2 Purchase price of major raw materials guaranteed throughout year. Annual requirements determined by sales forecast and inventory plans. Lower deliveries necessary in August due to incidence of holidays at supplier.

3 Increase in wage rates anticipated in May. Full production anticipated by May. Annual requirements determined by sales forecasts and inventory policies. Total amount is spread through the year on the basis of working days each month.

4 Annual salary award anticipated in October.

5 Allowance made for inflationary drift, establishment of new production facilities and holiday payments to direct operatives.

Exhibit 4 Wenman Plastics: Estimated Timing of Income and Expenditure during the year ending March 31, 1974. (figures in $'000s)

Question 4

Is $684 the maximum amount of deficit during the year? A month by month cash book method of analysis will reveal whether this is so or not and you are invited to produce such an analysis from the information given in Part I with the fuller details appearing in Exhibit 4.

Preparing the
Short-Term Forecast

If the case for cash forecasting has been made
(and, we hope, proven)
let us now turn to the mechanics
of preparing a short-term cash forecast.
A later chapter will deal with
the mechanics of longer-term forecasts.
In this chapter we will look at the content, format
and frequency of the short-term cash forecast,
the source of input information
and the basic assumptions that must be made.

3.1 THE OBJECT OF THE EXERCISE

Because cash flow is so vital to a firm's continued existence, and because it is to a large extent determined by management action, it cannot be left to chance but must be controlled. Towards this end, management must attempt to forecast if, when, for how long, and in what amounts either a cash deficit or a cash surplus might present itself. The initial object of preparing a short-term cash forecast is thus to reveal the forecast cash and bank balances at the end of each short-term control period, e.g. a month, throughout the forthcoming planning period, e.g. a year. This involves forecasting the cash inflows and cash outflows in each of these control periods and the example in Figure 3.1 demonstrates in both numerical and graphical form the outcome of the exercise. It also demonstrates the vital need for forecasting short term, as opposed to annual, movements: in the example there is little difference between the opening (+5) and closing (−5) cash balances but there is a significant deficit partway through the year.

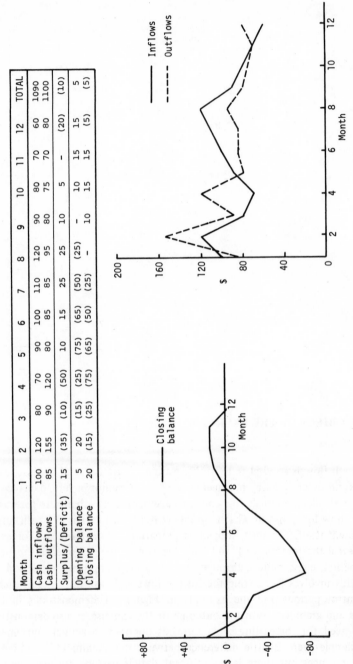

Month	1	2	3	4	5	6	7	8	9	10	11	12	TOTAL
Cash inflows	100	120	80	70	90	100	110	120	90	80	70	60	1090
Cash outflows	85	155	90	120	80	85	85	95	80	75	70	80	1100
Surplus/(Deficit)	15	(35)	(10)	(50)	10	15	25	25	10	5	-	(20)	(10)
Opening balance	5	20	(15)	(25)	(75)	(65)	(50)	(25)	-	10	15	15	5
Closing balance	20	(15)	(25)	(75)	(65)	(50)	(25)	-	10	15	15	(5)	(5)

Figure 3.1 Cash movement

But all of this is only the initial object of the exercise because it represents only a piece of clerical work. As such, it contributes nothing of real value to the well-being of the firm and is therefore only a means to an end rather than an end in itself.

The ultimate object of preparing the short-term cash forecast must be to guide appropriate and timely management action towards improved control of cash flow. This is where the value in a cash forecast lies. The action that management is able to take varies from time to time and as circumstances change, but it will always be directed towards one or more of the following ends:

1 Planning the management of future cash inflows and outflows so as to produce the most favorable control period closing balances.

2 Taking steps (in good time) to ensure that adequate financing is available as and when required to meet any anticipated cash deficit.

3 Taking steps (in good time) to ensure that any anticipated cash surplus is fully utilized to the maximum possible benefit to the firm.

4 Taking appropriate control action to maintain financial stability in the on-going situation as the actual cash flow position unfolds.

At this stage let us stay with the initial object of the exercise and review the steps through which the clerical effort must proceed in order to produce the short-term cash forecast. However let us never overlook the fact that this clerical effort must always be oriented towards the management action that subsequently might be taken.

3.2 FORMAT OF THE FORECAST

It is difficult to specify a precise format for a forecast because the action that management uses to control cash flow varies from industry to industry and from firm to firm. However, the action that management does take in the short term will almost certainly be directed towards specific items of cash receipt or cash payment and therefore the cash book method of analysis is recommended. The reader will recall that, as described in Chapter 2, the cash book method of analysis is the one that concentrates on individual receipts and payments; an example appeared in Figure 2.1 and is now reproduced in Figure 3.2 as a suggested framework for preparing a short-term forecast.

An early decision must be made as to the degree of detail that should be presented within the list of receipts and payments: the comments made in Section 2.2 when discussing the degree of detail necessary for historical analysis have equal relevance here. In short we are not concerned with attempting to forecast the flow of cash under every detailed subjective head of receipt and payment; rather we are concerned with rough cuts at groupings which will highlight the more significant items and particularly those items over which management is most able to exercise control. The framework suggested in Figure 3.2 should provide a degree of analysis that is appropriate in many situations, but of course it may require expansion or contraction to meet the needs of individual circumstances.

Another early decision concerns selection of both the planning horizon, i.e. how far ahead to plan, and the number of short-term control periods up to the planning horizon. The framework in Figure 3.2 has been drawn up with columns suggesting monthly control intervals within a one year planning cycle; these have been selected as being reasonably representative of business activity. The planning horizon should be sufficiently far ahead to take account of any significantly large once-per-annum item of receipt or payment and should also cover any anticipated seasonal swing—a shorter period could portray a distorted or unrepresentative picture. For these reasons one year is suggested: furthermore, management is thereby given the earliest possible warning of impending financial crises.

As far as the selection of short-term control periods is concerned, these should be as realistic and practical as possible. Many items of receipt and payment are settled on a monthly basis and for this reason monthly control periods are frequently selected. However, what must not be overlooked is that the forecasted closing cash and bank balance for each control period is the actual closing balance; it could be quite different at other times within the period. For this reason it is necessary not to have too long a control period because there might be no time to recover from a mid-point crisis: after all, the main reason why the annual plan is broken down into shorter control periods is to reveal how the cash is likely to flow *between* the beginning and end points. Therefore if the financial position is precarious in the immediate short term or if it is likely to be seriously affected by the erratic incidence of receipts and payments throughout the month, the monthly control interval may prove inadequate. In such circumstances it might be sensible to select weekly control intervals for, say, the first month and monthly intervals thereafter. Some firms may feel there is a declining need for short intervals as the forecast moves out in time and therefore might select columns on its forecasting format as follows:

1 Weekly for the first month.

2 Monthly thereafter for the first quarter.

3 Quarterly thereafter for the rest of the year.

Line No.		APL	MAY	JUN	JUL	AUG	SEP	OCT	NOV	DEC	JAN	FEB	MAR
	CASH RECEIPTS												
1	Collections from customers												
2	Cash sales												
	Miscellaneous:												
3	Routine, e.g. rent, interest												
4	Special, e.g. sale of assets												
5	TOTAL RECEIPTS (R)												
	CASH PAYMENTS												
6	Payments to suppliers												
7	Wages, salaries and labor-related exps												
8	Miscellaneous routine items												
9	Rent, telephone, electricity, rates												
10	Taxes												
11	Purchase of buildings, plant, equipment												
12	Interest and dividend payments												
13	Repayment of borrowings												
14	Special items												
15	TOTAL PAYMENTS (P)												
17	CURRENT SURPLUS (DEFICIT): (R − P)												
18	Cash and bank balances at end of previous month												
19	CASH AND BANK BALANCES AT END OF CURRENT MONTH												

Figure 3.2 Forecast of cash movements using the cash book method

The way in which the framework in Figure 3.2 is put together clearly suggests an individual monthly forecast of receipts and payments with a cumulative position shown at the foot. This is the authors' preference. An alternative approach used by some firms is to produce the whole forecast on a cumulative basis, e.g. the figures in the June column are cumulative to June, in the July column they are cumulative to July and so on. This has some advantages when considering the rate of cash receipts and payments throughout the year and when monitoring actual performance: the cumulative method of presentation may be worthy of consideration.

3.3   FREQUENCY OF FORECASTING

Because the planning cycle suggested is one year, this should not imply that preparation of a short-term cash forecast is an annual event. The overall planning, or budgeting for a firm is frequently done on an annual basis, perhaps with a budget revision at six-month intervals. A cash forecast will clearly form part of this annual budget process. In this way it will reflect the cash flow consequences of all the detailed budget decisions. However, the cash position is too vital to be left for annual or even six-month consideration. Once it has started its life in the annual budgeting routines, the cash forecast should thereafter be seen as a continuing responsibility in its own right.

Ideally, therefore, cash forecasting should be undertaken on a rolling basis monthly (or more frequently if shorter control periods are chosen). If the first forecast runs from April to March, the next will run from May to April, the next from June to May, and so on. Each succeeding forecast brings up another control period in the extreme right hand column. In this way, the earliest warning of impending crises is given and appropriate action can be planned by management rather than resorting to last minute panic measures.

If forecasting is undertaken on a monthly basis as suggested, a comparison of each month's column on succeeding forecasts can be quite revealing as to the quality of forecasting expertise or to the incidence of management's action plans. (For example, how does the forecast for October compare with the April, May, and June forecasts?) Obviously, if succeeding forecasts do not reveal significant changes in the figures for intervening months, there is good argument to reduce the frequency of making forecasts, for example from monthly intervals to perhaps bi-monthly or even quarterly intervals. However, in this case it is imperative that the underlying assumptions on which the forecast was based are monitored in the meantime in case an unexpected change of events creeps into the system and takes management by surprise. When financial trouble strikes, it is often not so much of the nature of the trouble itself which creates the difficulty for the firm but the speed with which management is able to recognize the situation and respond to it. Herein lies the greatest danger in reducing the interval between forecasts of future cash movements.

3.4 ANALYSIS OF PAST PERFORMANCE

Having determined the format, periodicity, and frequency of preparing the forecast, now comes the task of inserting the numbers! Forecasting certainly gets easier with practice but how does one accomplish the task for the first time? Perhaps the most important initial step is to ascertain how cash flow has behaved in the past. Therefore a useful starting position from which to develop the detail and figures to put into the cash forecast is to analyze past cash flows as described in Chapter 2, but using the identical framework and format as used in the forecast.

Let me hasten to stress that I do not suggest that cash forecasting is a blind extrapolation of past cash flows. It can be most dangerous to assume that the past will automatically repeat itself in the future! Nevertheless, when preparing a cash forecast, the availability of an analysis of past cash flows will be of invaluable assistance for the following reasons:

1 The behavior of cash flow in the firm will be brought into focus in a manner that has not, perhaps, been available before. (For example: What are the significant items? To what extent do they vary from month to month?)

2 Experience will be gained in performing that analysis of actual cash flows which will be required as the basis for monitoring future performance. It is pointless to select a basis of forecasting for which actual information cannot subsequently be provided.

3 Vital information on patterns of cause and effect relationship in cash flows, e.g. the average time delay in collection from customers, will be compiled.

4 Similarly, the effect on cash flow of specific management decisions can be traced, e.g. the decision to increase inventory levels.

Each of the above must be known to the forecaster when approaching the task. If they are already available then clearly an analysis of past cash flows is less necessary.

3.5 DIARY OF OCCURRENCES

If an analysis of past cash flows is deemed necessary to assist the preparation of a forecast, the ascertainment of cause and effect relationships in cash flows will be greatly facilitated if a diary of significant occurrences is compiled. The items to be recorded are those major external occurrences, e.g. annual and public holidays, strikes, imposition of government controls; or internal occurrences, e.g. introduction of shift working, fulfilling a large export order, which have a significant impact upon cash flow. An example of such a diary with suggested entries appears in Figure 3.3.

The diary will initially be used to assist the analysis of past cash flows. An apparently unexplainable receipt or payment or a sudden change in an otherwise regular pattern of cash flows might easily be explained by the impact of one or more of these occurrences. However, once the impact of occurrences has been isolated in this way it will provide valuable assistance to the correct incorporation of the impact of predictable occurrences, e.g. statutory holidays, into future forecasts. Furthermore, if the impact of unpredictable occurrences, e.g. a strike in the past, is isolated, this will provide valuable information in the evaluation and guidance of appropriate management action if or when a similar occurrence presents itself in the future.

3.6 FORECASTING ASSUMPTIONS

Not many managers are genuinely clairvoyant, and so forecasting does not come easily to them. In fact, a forecast is no more than someone's belief in the future based upon certain assumptions that have been made regarding future events. If the assumptions subsequently prove to be wrong, then the forecast will also be incorrect. For this reason, it is necessary to set down formally the key assumptions on which major parts of the forecast are based. Subsequently these assumptions will be monitored (in addition to monitoring the cash flows themselves) as a basis for giving management the earliest warning of impending financial difficulties.

In the same way that the diary of occurrences was an essential element in the analysis of past performance, so a similar "diary" should be maintained of critical assumptions made in compiling the forecast. Assumptions must be made both as to the occurrence of a key event and also as to its timing—the latter is often more critical than the former. The diary of forecasting assumptions is essentially similar in appearance to the diary of occurrences (Figure 3.3).

3.7 RELIABILITY OF PREDICTIONS

Let us be honest: perhaps the only thing that can be said with certainty about any forecast is that it is likely not to turn out exactly that way in actuality! But this fact of life should not detract from the value of a forecast. A forecast that

	APL	MAY	JUN	JUL	AUG	SEP	OCT	NOV	DEC	JAN	FEB	MAR
Statutory holidays:												
Easter												
Spring												
August												
Christmas												
Annual vacation or holiday shutdown												
Strikes:												
Own workers												
Major suppliers												
Major customers												
Important services												
National												
Cost inflation:												
Own wage rates												
Major suppliers												
Important services												
Own selling price increases												
Major events:												
Economic: Domestic												
Other												
Political: Domestic												
Other												
Significant indicators:												
Sales value of production												
Number of working days												
Index of retail prices												
Other												

Figure 3.3 Analysis of cash movements—diary of significant events

'. . .a forecast is no more than someone's belief in the future based upon certain assumptions which have been made regarding future events. . .'

turns out to be "wrong" is not necessarily a "bad" forecast. Remember that the ultimate objective of the exercise is to guide appropriate and timely management action toward improved control of cash flow. For this reason a "good" forecast is not the one that turns out to be "right" but the one that, as the future unfolds and diverges from the forecast itself, provides a sound basis for such management action.

In fact, there will be a mixture of degrees of reliability within a cash forecast because its preparation represents the assembly of the following components:

1 Forecasts based on known immediate past occurrences, for example the first month's collections from past sales or payments for past purchases, or known future occurrences (e.g. payment of tax liability, receipt of interest on a loan).

2 The impact of known current and intended future management decisions in those ten areas representing the major determinants of cash flow which were summarized in Section 1.7.

3 Knowledge of patterns of behavior and cause and effect relationships which were gained from the analysis of past performance.

4 Critical assumptions as to the incidence and timing of future performance and occurrences.

Clearly the earlier columns of each forecast will tend to be much more reliable, being nearer in time and having less uncertainty to handle. Later columns are less certain and thus can be used only as general guides. However, this type of quality in the information is, of course, quite appropriate to management's needs. More precise guidance is necessary for the more critical immediate future when time is not on the side of the management decision. The less immediate future is not as dependent on quick, short term management action and therefore does not require the same degree of precision in the information provided.

Thus, unreliability can be accommodated in a forecast and will not necessarily detract from its value provided that management is prepared to accept the fact of unreliability and react accordingly when making decisions. This is all that need be said at this stage but we shall return to the subject in a later chapter when we review several more sophisticated management approaches to uncertainty.

3.8 FORECASTING THE CASH FLOWS

We now turn to the actual process of putting numbers onto the suggested cash forecast form shown in Figure 3.2. Some numbers are less difficult to predict than others, for example, because they are more under control of management or because their amount or date of receipt or payment is fixed or relatively easy to predict. Forecasts must be realistic. For example, they must take inflationary trends into account where appropriate. As has been stressed elsewhere in this book, the forecast of timing is equally as important as the forecast of numbers themselves. The comments made above concerning reliability of predictions are clearly of importance when carrying out this task.

The derivation of the numbers for some of the lines on the forecast form will be readily apparent but a few brief comments of amplification may be appropriate in each case:

Line 1 *Collections from customers*—More detailed comments on this item are made in Section 3.9.

Line 2 *Cash sales*—This item can only be based upon sales forecasts tempered by past experience.

Lines 3 & 4 *Miscellaneous*—These items are matters of fact or management intention.

Line 6 *Payments to suppliers*—This item is compounded of sales and production plans, inventory policies, purchasing policy, the reliability of supplier delivery, and policy regarding length of credit taken from suppliers. What is more, different policies may be adopted toward different materials or toward different suppliers. For this reason, fairly extensive computations on a supporting schedule may be necessary. Clearly any anticipated price increases must be taken into account. This item in particular is one where declining reliability of the less immediate future forecasts is most pronounced and, therefore, is an item which should receive special attention at each monthly forecast.

Line 7 *Wages, salaries, etc.*—This item should not present too much difficulty even though it is a significant item. Anticipated patterns of shift, overtime or part-time working will be taken into account as will anticipated wage increases and salary reviews.

Line 8 *Miscellaneous*—This item will be guided to a considerable extent by past experience but inflationary trends must, of course, be taken into account.

Line 9 *Rent, telephone, etc.*—This item represents the aggregation, via a supporting schedule of those services where settlement is on a regular basis, perhaps quarterly, half yearly or yearly. Prediction should not present too much difficulty provided that price increases are taken into account where appropriate.

Line 10 *Taxes*—More detailed comments on this item are made below.

Lines 11 to 14 *Capital expenditures, financial obligations and special items*— These items are matters of fact or management intention. Supporting schedules will be prepared as necessary.

3.9   FORECAST COLLECTIONS FROM CUSTOMERS

Perhaps one of the more difficult items to predict—and yet perhaps the most critical to the performance of the firm—is the collections from customers. Here one tries to predict both the amount of sales invoiced and the length of time that will elapse before settlement, i.e. the collection period. Neither factor lies entirely in the complete control of management. Fortunately, however, in the first month or two of the forecast only one factor presents difficulty—the collection period. Sales have already been invoiced in respect of these collections and, what is more, the forward order book may permit a fairly accurate forecast of sales that are to be invoiced in the immediate future. Unfortunately, uncertainties as to sales and to collection period both increase as the forecast pushes out into the future. However the points made earlier regarding this declining reliability are particularly appropriate in this context.

In certain industries, specific contractual relationships regarding settlement exist with individual customers, e.g. building and contracting and equipment rental. In these circumstances the forecast of cash collections must take account of the predicted sales value of work done, the pattern of payment that will be negotiated, *and* the collection period which might be experienced. Particularly in the case of a building contractor, the forecast of cash collections may therefore have to be aggregated from forecasts for individual contracts which are being, or are to be, undertaken.

No doubt the majority of cases will not be of the type referred to in the previous paragraph but will be concerned with general sales invoicing to customers for payment on the expiration of credit terms which are regarded as 'normal' for industry. The anticipated collection period built into forecast collections from such customers will be based upon target credit levels that the firm intends to achieve. But it is essential that these are realistic and take into account both past experience and any peculiar mix of either sales or customers. In this context the analysis of past performance will provide vital evidence on the pattern of past credit experience. A form similar to Figure 3.4 will be of assistance in attempting to isolate any pattern that might exist. A stable overall pattern might emerge relatively easily from this form but if such a pattern does not readily present itself it will be necessary to undertake a more detailed analysis. The more detailed analysis would certainly be necessary for example if different credit terms were allowed to different classes of customers or even to one or two individual but significantly large customers, either domestic or foreign. If significant differences between classes of customers or individual customers exist, then a shift in their relative mix within any month's sales will clearly cause imbalance in future collections. The anticipated sales mix must therefore be taken into account, perhaps by using subsidiary schedules to build up the total forecast collections from customers.

3.10 CASH FLOW AND TAXES

The incidence of tax payment bears quite heavily upon the cash position of the firm. Indeed certain elements of tax legislation may have been introduced with the specific objective of controlling liquidity. The incidence of tax payments is therefore an important factor when compiling the cash forecast. Each country has its own tax regulations—both local and national, both based on profits and on other factors—and clearly a complete review of such regulations is beyond the scope of this book. However those beginning the compilation of a cash forecast must appraise themselves of local legislation. Merely to demonstrate the importance of the subject, a brief excursion will be made into two United Kingdom examples: Corporation Tax and Value Added Tax.

Month	Sales invoiced $	Averages sales/day $	Collections outstanding at month end $	Average no. days sales outstanding Days	Percentage of sales collected within:			
					1 month %	2 months %	3 months %	Over 3 mths %
April								
May								
June								
July								
August								
September								
October								
November								
December								
January								
February								
March								

Figure 3.4 Analysis of cash movements—collections from customers

United Kingdom Corporation Tax is calculated on the statutory income of a company and is payable to a pattern also determined by statute. Statutory income represents profit that has been declared by the company but somewhat adjusted and then subjected to certain statutory deductions: a series of reliefs and allowances, the most important of which is capital allowances, representing a considerably accelerated depreciation charge. In fact, the capital allowance, on certain types of expenditure or in certain parts of the country where capital expenditure is being encouraged, may amount to a 100 per cent write-off in the first year. Clearly, it follows that the total tax liability may bear no relationship to the profits declared by the company. In fact, it is quite possible for the tax liability to be nil despite the existence of profits. The *computation* of corporate tax liability thus affects cash flow and should be considered independently of the date of payment.

The date of payment of United Kingdom Corporation Tax is also quite important. Basically this is a date nine months after the end of the fiscal year but for many companies some old tax rules still apply, whereby the tax is due and payable January 1, which can be a minimum of nine months (for companies whose year ends on March 31) to a maximum of twenty-one months (for companies whose year ends on April 30) after the end of the fiscal year. This granting of credit by the government is clearly advantageous to cash flow. However, superimposed upon this basic pattern is ACT or Advance Corporation Tax. If a company pays a dividend to its shareholders then, within two weeks of the end of the quarter during which the dividend was paid, an amount that varies with the size of the dividend must be handed over to the government as an advance payment of the corporation tax that will next fall due for payment. The rules for computation of corporation tax can be in conflict with the rules for payment. For example a company may have a nil tax liability due to the incidence of statutory reliefs or allowances but still find itself paying ACT if it declares a dividend.

The unrelieved ACT can of course be carried forward until there is a corporation tax liability against which it can be offset, but in the meantime the company has suffered a considerable acceleration in its cash outflow on taxation.

United Kingdom Value Added Tax (VAT)* is calculated at a statutory rate on the invoice value of certain taxable classes of goods or services called output tax. At the same time, VAT will be added to the invoice value of certain goods or services purchased by a firm called input tax. Periodically (normally every quarter), the difference between the input and output tax will be paid over to

---

*A Value Added Tax (VAT) is a national sales tax system. A VAT system taxes each stage in the processing and marketing of a product until it reaches the consumer. Under this system, a tax is placed on the costs and profits of each stage and all the value added taxes are rolled up to the consumer. The European Community member countries (i.e., Belgium, Denmark, France, Ireland, Italy, Luxembourg, the Netherlands, the United Kingdom, and West Germany) have adopted a VAT system and other countries are considering adopting such a system.

	Period 1	Period 2
	$	$
VAT added to sales invoiced	1000	900
Vat added to cost of goods and services consumed	300	950
Settlement with Customs & Excise:		
VAT to be paid over	700	
VAT recoverable		50

Figure 3.5

or claimed back from (as the case may be) the Customs and Excise. The simple example in Figure 3.5 demonstrates the mechanics. The net effect of all this is that the final impact of VAT is pushed down the line to the ultimate consumer who is not entitled to reclaim any VAT he has suffered.

Whether the firm is a net payer to, or net recipient from, the Customs and Excise clearly affects the pattern of forecast cash receipts and payments. However, VAT has a more subtle impact upon cash flows. Note that it is calculated on *invoices,* not upon cash flows. This means that the total cash flow on VAT is a function not only of the periodic settlement with Customs and Excise but also of normal credit terms granted to customers or taken from suppliers. Clearly it could be possible for a firm to have to hand over VAT on sales invoiced before it has in fact made the cash collection from its customers—and of course vice versa with VAT on invoices from its suppliers. A specimen calculation of forecast cash flows on VAT is incorporated into the Wenman Plastics case study at the end of this chapter—see Exhibit 6.

3.11 PLANNED MANAGEMENT DECISIONS

On completion, the forecast may reveal a cash position some time during the forthcoming planning period which is unacceptable to management. Figure 3.6 shows a movement of cash balances to demonstrate the point. If the broken line represents the maximum cash deficit permitted by existing bank facilities then situation B is acceptable but situation A is unacceptable. If the unacceptable situation is to be avoided, management must clearly reconsider some of the decisions that were built into this forecast and develop future action plans that will accelerate certain receipts or delay certain payments sufficiently to restructure the forecast and produce an acceptable pattern of future cash flow. The action plans that are available to management in these circumstances are essentially similar to the actions that would be taken to restore an adverse actual cash position in the ongoing situation. For this reason, full discussion is delayed

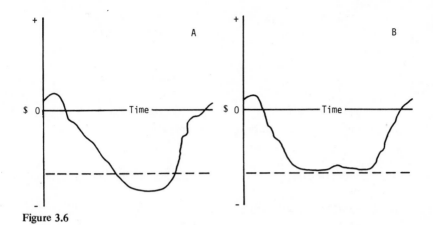

Figure 3.6

until the next chapter which is concerned with monitoring and controlling actual performance. Decisions that management knows it must take some months in the future can be carefully planned and they are more likely to be rational and logical than last minute panic measures taken in the face of a rapidly deteriorating ongoing situation.

However, despite all the careful development of management plans and the monitoring of cash forecasts, something may still go wrong and precipitate an unexpected cash crisis. What will management do then? Ideally and quite simply, management should at that time select from a carefully prepared schedule of planned actions which were tabulated in advance just in case the unexpected did happen. This implies the development of carefully-thought-through contingency plans, and this process should logically form the final stage of cash forecasting. Again this ensures that actions which management might have to take in the future represent a planned rather than a panic response. The subject of contingency planning will also be covered in a later chapter and so will be taken no further here.

3.12 SUMMARY

In this chapter we have looked at the mechanics of preparing the short-term forecast. Let us conclude with a summary of the steps that will be necessary in undertaking this exercise:

1 Determine the framework for the forecast:
    a. the degree of detail necessary,
    b. the planning horizon,

    c. the duration of control periods,

    d. the frequency with which the forecast shall be prepared.

2 Obtain historical data if not already available:

    a. analyze past cash flows using the same framework selected for the forecast,

    b. analyze cause and effect relationships, e.g. credit collection periods,

    c. compile a diary of significant occurrences.

3 Predict the future:

    a. forecast the cash receipts and cash payments in the manner determined at (1) above,

    b. set down significant assumptions.

4 Reflect, reconsider, and plan accordingly:

    a. restructure the forecast if necessary,

    b. develop a short list of contingent management actions to meet emergencies that might arise.

Wenman Plastics:
Part 3

Please note that all amounts are expressed to the nearest $1000. Readers are first invited to review Part 2 of this case study and to compare their own cash forecasts (produced in response to Questions 3 and 4) with those which appear as Exhibits 5 and 6 in this part of the study.

Claude Wenman was aware that if he wished to reveal exactly how the forecast cash deficit had arisen at March 31, 1974, the simplest method was to follow through each of the balance sheet items from March 31, 1973 to March 31, 1974. Whereas it was simple in the majority of cases, certain items (for example, fixed assets, tax, and dividend) represented the combined effect of true cash movements and accounting adjustments. In such cases, it was necessary to 'unscramble' the accounting adjustment in order to reveal the pure impact on cash movement. Having thus completed his calculations, Claude was able to produce the analysis of total forecast cash movements which is reproduced as Exhibit 5.

He was surprised to see that the increase in inventories and customer credit which were necessary to service the anticipated level of sales had had such a

	$'000s	$'000s
INFLOWS OF CASH		
Operations before tax (potential cash flow from operations: Exhibit 2)	795	
New sources of capital:		
Secured loan	450	
Additional supplier credit	270	
Liquidation of surplus assets: sale of short-term investments	100	1615
OUTFLOWS OF CASH		
Tax payment	150	
Dividend payment	100	
Interest payment	72	
Acquisition of assets:		
Purchase of fixed assets	1000	
Increase in inventories	555	
Additional customer credit	432	2309
Total deficit over year to March 31,1974		694
Bank balances and cash March 31,1973		10
Deficit at March 31, 1974 (as Exhibits 3 and 6)		$684

Note: the amounts shown above have generally been obtained by tracing the movements that have taken place in individual items between Exhibits 1 and 3.

Exhibit 5 Wenman Plastics—analysis of total forecast cash movements, year to March 31, 1974

considerable impact upon the position. He thought about his inventory policy which had determined the safety levels of inventory he would carry and he also pondered the impact of his production policy. Clearly March 31 would not represent the month of highest inventory. Similarly, March 31 would not represent the month of peak debtors or receivables.

There now seemed to be even greater need to prepare the alternative analysis which would reveal the cash inflows and outflows on a monthly basis throughout the year ending March 31, 1974. Armed with the estimates he had already made, Claude was able to produce the monthly cash flow forecast which is reproduced as Exhibit 6.

He was pleased to see that the ultimate deficit shown in the extreme right hand column was the same $684 which had already appeared in his forecast balance sheet (Exhibit 3) and in his analysis of total forecast cash movements (Exhibit 5). However, he was dismayed to notice that, as he had feared, this was by no means the peak deficit. In fact, it ranged from a low $21 at the end of April to a high $1082 at the end of October (there was the possibility of course that the deficit could be even higher than this *during* October). So Claude had to face one of two alternatives if he were to go ahead with his project without risk of financial disaster:

1 He must secure additional funds in the pattern of amounts indicated by the final line of Exhibit 6.

	Apl	May	Jun	Jul	Aug	Sep	Oct	Nov	Dec	Jan	Feb	Mar
CASH RECEIPTS												
Collections from customers[1]	200	400	250	250	350	400	200	500	800	500	500	500
Secured loan received	450											
Sale of short-term invest.	100											
TOTAL RECEIPTS	750	400	250	250	350	400	200	500	800	500	500	500
CASH PAYMENTS												
Payments to suppliers[2]	50	50	110	200	200	250	50	150	200	200	150	200
Labor[3]	78	153	136	136	102	102	170	136	102	170	136	119
Salaries and related exps[3]	38	38	38	38	38	38	42	42	42	42	42	42
Rent, rates, elec. & 'phone[3]	110			80			75			135		
Other running expenses[3]	30	44	27	30	93	62	30	32	66	33	33	50
Additional plant, equipment and vehicles[3]	400	400				100				50		50
Interest on secured loan[3]			18			18			18			18
Ordinary dividend[3]	50						50					
Corporation tax[4]		25						25		100		
Value added tax net outflow (inflow)[5]	25	5	(54)	1	(11)	34	(7)	(26)	45	(13)	(26)	39
TOTAL PAYMENTS	781	715	275	485	422	604	410	359	473	717	335	518
MONTHLY SURPLUS (DEFICIT)	(31)	(315)	(25)	(235)	(72)	(204)	(210)	141	327	(217)	165	(18)
Cash and bank balances at end of previous month	10	(21)	(336)	(361)	(596)	(668)	(872)	(1082)	(941)	(614)	(831)	(666)
CASH AND BANK BALANCES AT END OF CURRENT MONTH	(21)	(336)	(361)	(596)	(668)	(872)	(1082)	(941)	(614)	(831)	(666)	(684)

Notes

[1]April and May represent collection of sundry debtors (accounts receivable) at March 31,1973: thereafter each month's collections represent sales two months previously (see Exhibit 4 and also credit terms referred to in Part 1).

Exhibit 6 Wenman Plastics—monthly cash flow forecast, year to March 31, 1974 (figures in $'000s)

Exhibit 6, continued

2April and May represent payment of sundry creditors (accounts payable) at March 31,1973 : thereafter each month's payments represent purchases two months previously (see Exhibit 4 and also the credit terms referred to in Part 1).

3See Exhibit 4.

4The total payment of $150 is the current tax appearing in the balance sheet as at March 31,1973. Advance Corporation Tax (ACT) payments will be made in May and November arising from the Ordinary dividend payments in April and October.

5In practice this item would not appear in this manner but is shown thus to demonstrate the combined impact of value-added tax and credit settlement terms on cash movements. The detailed calculation of the amount shown is:

	Apl	May	Jun	Jul	Aug	Sep	Oct	Nov	Dec	Jan	Feb	Mar
"Output tax", i.e. VAT added to sales invoices	(20)	(20)	(28)	(32)	(16)	(40)	(64)	(40)	(40)	(40)	(16)	(64)
"Input tax", i.e. VAT added to purchase invoices	9	16	16	20	4	12	16	16	12	16	16	12
Estimate of VAT included in other payments for taxable good or services	37	33	2	5	1	10	5	2	2	11	2	6
NET VAT RECOVERABLE (PAYABLE)	26	29	(10)	(7)	(11)	(18)	(43)	(22)	(26)	(13)	2	(46)
Quarterly settlement of VAT: receipt (payment)			45			(36)			(91)			(57)
Collection of VAT added to sales invoices (see note 1 above)	16	32	20	20	28	32	16	40	64	40	40	40
Payment of VAT added to purchase invoices (see note 2 above)	(4)	(4)	(9)	(16)	(16)	(20)	(4)	(12)	(16)	(16)	(12)	(16)
Payment of VAT included in other items	(37)	(33)	(2)	(5)	(1)	(10)	(5)	(2)	(2)	(11)	(2)	(6)
NET EFFECT ON MONTHLY CASH INFLOW (OUTFLOW)	(25)	(5)	54	(1)	11	(34)	7	26	(45)	13	26	(39)

In practice only the quarterly settlement would be shown separately on the cash forecast; the other three items would be incorporated automatically into the collections from customers, payments to suppliers, etc., in the appropriate line of the cash forecast.

2 He must reconsider the decisions which he or his father had made or were proposing to make and which were summarized in Part 1 of this case study. Hopefully a change in some or all of these decisions might reduce the deficit without creating too much damage to either sales or profit.

Question 5

Look once more at the list of decisions which you tabulated in response to Question 1 (see Part 1). Does Claude have scope for changing any of these decisions in such a way as to reduce the total cash deficit without seriously affecting his sales or profit?

In each case, try to assess the possible impact that such a change might have upon the cash position and also the extent to which such a change would appeal to either Karl or Claude Wenman.

Question 6

What action would you advise Claude to take?

Monitoring
and Controlling
Cash Flow

*The cash forecast is, of course, a clerical exercise
and as such can contribute nothing
to improved liquidity or cash control in the firm.
Only management action can affect liquidity—
for good or ill! In this chapter we now turn
to the necessary monitoring of performance
which must be undertaken
and suggest some of the actions
that management might take
to control and improve cash flow.
Many such actions in an ongoing situation
are in the working capital area,
and so we shall devote much of the chapter
to this specific area.*

4.1 SCOPE FOR MANAGEMENT ACTION

We made the point at the beginning of Chapter 3 that the ultimate object of preparing a short-term cash forecast is to guide appropriate and timely management action towards improved control of cash flow. Indeed, if the cash forecast is undertaken as an isolated clerical exercise and then completely and quietly laid to rest in the corporate archives, it will have represented nothing more than an expensive clerical exercise with little or no real value to the firm beyond perhaps the creation for the first time of an awareness of the behavior of cash flow. Not an encouraging epitaph! Clearly the benefits of cash forecasting, which were tabulated in an earlier chapter, cannot be reaped merely by wanting them. Figures of themselves do nothing—only management action can get results.

The action that management is able to take falls broadly into two categories:

1 Action to develop a more tolerable forecast (with respect to either size or duration) of the cash and bank balances throughout some future period.

91

2 Action to correct an ongoing situation that is getting out of hand—as revealed by a comparison of actual and forecast cash and bank balances at any point in time.

Action taken in either category is essentially similar because each is striving to achieve the same end: namely to improve the liquidity position of the firm. However the initiation of the two categories of action is quite different. The first category implies timely forethought which will generate more specific action planning; the second category implies expedient actions taken quickly in an ongoing situation which very often is rapidly changing. The essence of the difference between the two categories is timeliness. In the second category, time is not on the side of the decision maker and, therefore, there is a clear possibility that action taken under this category will not be thought through quite so clearly as the decision taken under the first category. For this reason, action in the second category could in reality amount to nothing more than hasty panic measures which might do more harm than good. To avoid these worst consequences of the category two decision it is advantageous for management to have available a short list of carefully thought through contingency plans from which to select in case of need. Thus the action in the second category can also be made the subject of timely forethought via systematic contingency planning (a subject that will be taken up in greater detail in a later chapter).

Specific management control action that can be taken under either of the above categories at a particular point in time will of course be constrained by circumstances ruling at the time the decision is taken. For example, the nature and size of the cash problem, the financial standing of the firm, the industrial environment and state of the market, the general economic climate, availability and cost of financing—all can dictate what is and what is not acceptable or possible. For this reason it is not realistic to set down a hard and fast list of recommended foolproof, fail-safe steps for improving the cash position of any firm, under any circumstances, overnight. However it is possible to highlight the basic principles that should be followed in initiating management action that seeks to change the cash and bank balances for the better. Let us first turn our attention to these principles and later review a few examples of potential management actions.

4.2 NATURE OF MANAGEMENT ACTION

In Chapter 2 we discussed the cash tank method of analyzing cash movements and a schematic diagram of a cash flow system was shown in Figure 2.4. Reflection upon this diagram will make clear that the action which management must take to redeploy a cash surplus or to counteract a cash deficit consists of closing down some or all of the outlet valves and/or opening up some or all of the inlet valves, bearing in mind that the amount, duration, and rate of flow can differ quite considerably from pipe to pipe. Thus Figure 2.4 gives a simple overview of the scope for management action that can be taken either to develop a more tolerable forecast or to correct an ongoing situation.

When selecting which valve to activate, the first and essential basic principle must be that any action taken should avoid, or at least minimize, damage to the future of the firm. For example, one action that can dramatically improve the cash position simply is to stop paying suppliers. *But* what does this do to the corporate image, to relations with suppliers, and to the guarantee of future deliveries? A similarly simple action which can be taken is to stop immediately any further expenditure on either maintenance or advertising. *But* how long before the factory grinds to a halt or the order intake declines to a dangerous level?

Before initiating any action designed to correct the cash position, management should attempt to assess its impact on the future of the firm. How far will the ripples spread once the stone is tossed into the pool? To this end, it may be useful to consider the following types of management actions.

4.2.1 Time-Related Actions

These are actions to bring forward cash inflows or to delay cash outflows but not necessarily to change their amount, e.g. speeding up collections from customers, delaying payments to suppliers and others, and postponing capital expenditures. These actions are self-correcting over time. All they do is change the time pattern of cash flows and thus they will not significantly affect future performance of the firm.

4.2.2 Volume-Related Actions

Decisions to change the volume of operations automatically result in changes in cash flow (complete elimination of such operations is considered in Section 4.2.4). Examples are short time working in production and curtailment of sales. The impact these actions have on the future of the company depends on the degree of change and the length of time before a more normal policy is resumed.

4.2.3 Scale-Related Actions

These are changes in policy relating to the degree of commitment to a specific course of action, e.g. the levels of inventory to be carried; the amount to be spent on marketing, research, and development, or capital expenditure; the amount to be paid out to shareholders by way of dividend. These actions could have a considerable impact upon future performance depending on the incidence and depth of cut and the duration of the policy change.

4.2.4 Once-Off, One-Time Actions

These actions are irreversible policy decisions creating significant, discrete, once-off, nonrecurring cash flows, e.g. raising new capital, or significant divestments by liquidation of assets. Such actions again could have a considerable impact upon the future. What is more, they differ from the other three groups in that they represent the passing of a point of no return whereas decisions under the other groups can be reversed more simply.

Although the above groups have been considered from the point of view of correcting a cash deficit, management could be facing the alternative problem of a cash surplus. In this event, as we shall see below, the same grouping of management action applies and similar comments are appropriate, but in reverse, the underlying tests again would be the impact on the future performance of the firm and the facility with which the decision could be reversed if necessary.

Chapter 1 described the differences between profits and cash flow and reminded us of the need for management to be aware of both. It is perhaps worth mentioning here that management actions aimed at an improvement in the cash position must ultimately have their impact upon profits. Ideally, the one decision will enhance both profits and cash flow simultaneously; however the situation could arise (particularly with actions as described in Sections 4.2.2 and 4.2.4) where action designed to enhance cash flow unfortunately has the effect of impairing profits either immediately or in the future. Therefore, when taking any action designed to improve the cash position of the firm, wise management will also consider the impact that such action will have upon the profit position of the firm.

4.3 INFORMATION FOR CONTROL

The facility with which management is able to initiate action under either of the two broad categories discussed earlier in this chapter will be greatly assisted by the availability of appropriate and timely control information. Towards this end a monthly liquidity report will no doubt prove helpful to management. The contents of such a report need to be tailored to the specific requirements of individual management groups, but it is suggested that the contents should incorporate at least the following:

1 A schedule, prepared in exactly the same format as that used for forecasting cash flows, which monitors performance by revealing how the actual results compare to those forecast. Such a schedule would compare actual with forecast outcome, line by line, and point up favorable or adverse variances that had arisen.

2 A further schedule which monitors the major critical assumptions that have formed the basis for predicting future cash flows. A change in conditions surrounding any one of these key assumptions, despite the fact that it might have no effect on the immediate cash position, could have considerable impact in the future and is often the earliest warning of impending financial difficulties. For example, an engineering company, at the time of preparing its cash forecast, may have assumed that there would be no significant increase in the price of steel (its major raw material) before June 1. An announcement by the steel supplier on February 15, giving one month's notice of a 12 percent increase clearly will affect future cash flows.

3 Some means of monitoring forecasting expertise. If the forecast is prepared on a monthly basis, it could be useful to reveal how the forecaster's view of the month under review has changed as each succeeding forecast was prepared. This information is not only designed to enable management to form an opinion as to the quality of forecasting expertise. It will also highlight the frequency and incidence of exceptional or unexpected items that have had a critical impact on cash flow. In addition, it will help to indicate whether it is necessary to maintain the frequency of forecasting. If succeeding months do not reveal significant differences between forecasts, there may be justification for reducing this frequency.

4 Routine supporting schedules as necessary to reveal greater detail or to provide other additional information regarding significant items on the forecast versus actual comparison schedule referred to in (1) above. Items that might justify such treatment are, for example:

    a. Collections from customers—a schedule reporting current credit experience, or collection period, major overdue accounts, and bad debts, will provide most useful information to management.

    b. Payments to suppliers—a similar schedule reporting current experience on credit taken, discount given, and major overdue accounts.

    c. Inventory levels—a schedule comparing planned and actual levels of the more significant items of stock and work in progress can be most helpful when seeking reasons for cash flow problems.

5 A brief narrative report, incorporating nonroutine supporting schedules as necessary, giving such explanations, information, and detail as will assist diagnosis and decision making. In addition to commenting on significant variances, the report might incorporate information on capital expenditure progress, location of cash and bank balances, available bank borrowing facilities not yet taken up, and availability of short-term investments.

The example reproduced in Figure 4.1 demonstrates one form that the liquidity report might take.

When reporting on cash flow variances it is often helpful to differentiate between timing variances and other variances. Timing variances represent differences between forecast and actual cash flows which have been brought about simply because an individual item has actually been received or paid earlier or later than forecast. This type of variance will automatically right itself with the passage of time and, while its existence is important in the measurement of cash flow, action by management is either unnecessary or vastly different from that which needs to be taken on variances which do not reflect merely an error in forecasting timing. Firms that prepare their forecasts on a cumulative or moving annual total basis claim that timing variances are more conveniently accommodated by the periodic reporting of actual performance on the same cumulative or moving annual basis.

4.4 DEALING WITH A CASH SURPLUS

While a cash surplus perhaps presents a more acceptable problem than a cash deficit, it nevertheless requires considered management action. Again this action is directed either towards the development of a more tolerable forecast or to the correction of an ongoing situation. In either case, a surplus is not necessarily a good thing because the amount of the surplus in effect indicates the amount of underutilization of resources by the firm. A cash surplus, unless beneficially employed can only detract from the overall rate of return currently being earned by the firm on its total capital employed.

If the surplus is actually retained in cash it will earn precisely nothing (indeed it is likely to fall in value due to the eroding effect of inflation). On the other hand, if it is placed on deposit with the firm's bankers it might perhaps earn a nominal rate of return through the interest, if any, that is paid. But surely management ought to be able to deploy the surplus to greater benefit than that earned from bank interest. Let us consider some potential management actions that might be taken. Inevitably, circumstances alter cases and so only general suggestions can be made. Much depends upon the size of the cash surplus, the period of time for which it is available, and the degree of notice that management had that the cash surplus was becoming available. However, the following actions might be worth considering and reference is made to the four groups of management action tabled in Sections 4.2.1–4.2.4.

HARTLEY ENTERPRISES LIMITED

Liquidity Report for month of July 1979

Page 1 - Summary

1 End of month position

| | Current month | | Next month forecast $ |
	Forecast $	Actual $	
Cash and bank balances			
Outstanding debtors (receivables)			
Inventories			
Outstanding creditors (payables)			
Short-term investments			
Bank facilities (credit) not used			

2 Changes in key assumptions

Original assumption	Current experience

3 Comments

Figure 4.1 Part 1

HARTLEY ENTERPRISES LIMITED

Liquidity Report for month of July 1979

Page 2 - Forecast versus Actual Cash Movements

Line no.		Previous forecasts made in		Current fore-cast	Actual	Variance*	
		April $	May $	$	$	Better $	Worse $
	CASH RECEIPTS						
1	Collections from customers						
2	Cash sales						
	Miscellaneous:						
3	Routine						
4	Special						
5	TOTAL RECEIPTS (R)						
	CASH PAYMENTS						
6	Payments to suppliers						
7	Wages, salaries and labor-related expenses						
8	Miscellaneous routine items						
9	Rent, telephone, electricity and rates						
10	Taxes						
11	Purchase of buildings, plant and equipment						
12	Interest and dividend payments						
13	Repayment of borrowings						
14	Special items						
15	TOTAL PAYMENTS (P)						
17	CURRENT SURPLUS (DEFICIT) (R − P)						
18	Cash and bank balances at end of previous month						
19	CASH AND BANK BALANCES AT END OF CURRENT MONTH						

*Variances marked thus are timing variances: these have been brought about by changes in the date of receipt or payment and will automatically right themselves with the passage of time.

Figure 4.1 Part 2

HARTLEY ENTERPRISES LIMITED

Liquidity Report for month of July 1979

Page 3 - Collections from Customers

1 Average number of weeks sales outstanding

	Domestic	Export	Total
Current month			
Previous month			

2 Summary of outstanding amounts, current month

	Domestic		Export		Total
	%	$	%	$	$
One month					
Two months					
Three months*					
Over three months*					
Intercompany balances					
TOTAL	100		100		

3 Schedule of amounts outstanding three months and over*

Customer	Outstanding		Action taken	Comment
	$	Months		

4 Bad debts written off

Customer	$	Comment

Figure 4.1 Part 3

99

HARTLEY ENTERPRISES LIMITED

Liquidity Report for month of July 1979

Page 4 - Inventories
        Payments to Suppliers

1 Inventory levels on hand

	Forecast $	Actual $	%	Average weeks on hand	Last month actual $	Movement during month $
Raw materials						
Work in progress						
Finished goods						
Consignment stock						
Maintenance and production spares						
Fuel						
Consumable and other supplies						
TOTAL			100			

Comments

2 Summary of creditors (payables) outstanding

	Comments	$
Trade payables:		
One month		
Two months		
Three months		
Over three months		
Other payables		
TOTAL		
Average number of weeks purchases outstanding		

Figure 4.1 Part 4

100

1 If the cash surplus is likely to be available permanently, or for an extended period of time, then steps should be taken to deploy it profitably within the business if at all possible, perhaps by bringing forward a *planned* phase of re-equipment, expansion, or addition to the product range. It must be stressed that the cash surplus presents an opportunity for bringing forward something from the waiting list of already evaluated plans. It should not be recklessly squandered on harebrained, unprofitable schemes just because it happens to be available. (Here we have examples of time- and volume-rated actions.)

2 If the surplus is available for a shorter period of time, several formal short-term investment opportunities present themselves, e.g. investments with national and local governments, term deposits with banks, even overnight lending to the money market earns a useful return. Any rate of return is better than none, but it is important that this type of investment be both secure and easily liquidated at a predetermined date. Short-term cash surpluses should never be used for speculative investments nor for investments that cannot be liquidated in short term. (Here we have examples of time-related actions.)

3 Several other more obvious time-related actions present themselves as an alternative means of dealing with a short-term cash surplus, e.g. the earlier payment of amounts owing to suppliers and the earlier purchase of materials. Any action of this type should be undertaken only after careful evaluation of the implied equivalent per annum rate of return for such "investment." Discount may be offered by suppliers for prompt payment, indeed the firm may presently be losing cash discounts by not paying promptly. Note that if normal payment is extended to two months but 2½ percent is offered for prompt payment, then because this 2½ percent is being earned by accelerating settlement by two months, it represents 2½ × 6 or 15 percent per annum. This is a useful return for the short-term investment of surplus cash. Similarly, by taking delivery of materials earlier, it may be possible to negotiate a concessionary price with the supplier should it be to his advantage to deliver early. It may even be possible to avoid an anticipated price increase by early delivery. After taking account of any genuine out-of-pocket costs incurred by taking early delivery, it is possible again to work out the equivalent per annum rate of return represented by the net savings earned by this transaction.

4 If the cash surplus is permanent and no alternative use presents itself then perhaps early repayment of loans or other capital should be considered as a last resort. The rate of return earned on this use of the surplus cash is, of course, the amount saved in future interest on the capital repaid. (Quite clearly this is an example of a once-off, or one-time action.)

The cash forecast will sometimes enable a segmentation of the surplus into different amounts which are available for redeployment over different time scales. Consider Figure 4.2 which shows a forecast cash profile, or movement in cash balances. Areas A to E present distinctly different opportunities for deployment of the cash surplus represented by the total area above the horizontal axis of this graph. Area A for example represents the maximum amount that can be deployed for the longest period of time.

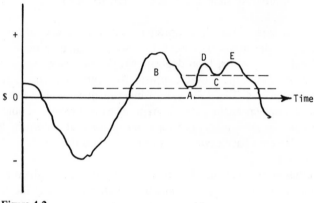

Figure 4.2

4.5 DEALING WITH A CASH DEFICIT

The existence of, or the anticipation of, a cash deficit does not automatically imply a search for additional financing from outside the firm. Management's initial response should always be to attempt to eliminate or to reduce the deficit by finer internal control of the valves on the cash tank. When we were considering how to deal with a cash surplus, we looked at the rate of return that could be earned by alternative methods of redeployment. Similarly, we should consider the cost of alternative ways of dealing with a deficit. Internal management action could come much more cheaply than a new external source of financing. Even if an external source has to be found, this might only be seen as a bridging operation pending the ability to bring on-stream an alternative internal source.

As with the cash surplus, so with the deficit. The size, duration, and degree of warning of the occurrence are critical factors in the selection of appropriate management action—be it time-related, volume-related, scale-related, or once-off (one-time). However, let us consider some specific actions that might be taken without the need to get involved in major volume- or scale-related cuts in levels of activity or expense, and without any large scale divestments. As a framework for discussion, reference is made to the line numbers employed on the form used both for our cash book method of cash forecasting and for the schedule comparing actual and forecast cash movements in the monthly liquidity report (see Figure 3.2 and Part 2 of Figure 4.1). This is the form that would be placed before management in order to reveal the need for action to deal with a cash deficit.

Line 1 *Collections from customers*—Is it possible, either over the whole range of customers or in the specific case of certain significant customers, to accelerate the rate of cash collections? The amount to be collected is a function of sales invoiced and the collection period. Leaving aside the question of sales volume, can anything be done to speed up the delay between dispatch of goods and collection of cash? Administrative activities concerned with invoicing, presentation of statements or other demands to the customer, control over the collection period, and the mechanics of cash collection and banking should each be put under the microscope to confirm that no unnecessary delay has crept in. One day's delay in presenting an invoice could delay cash inflow by one month if the invoice thereby fails to get into the customer's current accounting period. Checks collected by travelling sales representatives do nothing to ease the liquidity position until they are deposited at the bank.

Generally speaking the use of cash discounts to accelerate cash collections should be avoided because the cost of such action could be considerable. Similar comments were made above when considering whether to take cash discounts from suppliers. A discount of 2½ percent offered to accelerate collections by two months is equivalent to 15 percent per annum; acceleration by only one month costs 12 × 2½ percent or 30 percent per annum. This is an expensive means of raising funds. Moreover there is no guarantee that certain unscrupulous customers might not both take the discount *and* extend their payment period. This often results in unpleasant and protracted correspondence which might or might not result in recovery of the incorrectly taken discount.

Line 3 *Rents and interest received*—It may be possible to renegotiate terms in such a way as to have an accelerating effect on cash inflows either by earlier or more frequent settlements.

Line 4 *Sale of assets*—Without considering large scale divestment of activities, management should certainly review its current deployment of funds into either fixed assets, inventories, or other short-term deposits. Are there any individual items that represent redundant assets, the ongoing rate of return of which no longer justifies retention of the realizable values locked up in them? Many of us are squirrels at heart and prefer to hoard rather than divest. But by so doing we could be denying ourselves the opportunity of cash inflows with a very low price tag (in terms of current earnings foregone) and relying instead on an alternative source which is much more costly.

Line 6 *Payments to suppliers*—Warning was given earlier in this chapter regarding the indiscriminate curtailment of payments to suppliers and this is not to be recommended. However it may be possible to negotiate extended credit terms, either generally, or specifically with certain suppliers, or for certain commodities. Alternatively, new sources of supply may be sought which offer better terms. The value in interest saved arising from better credit terms may even justify payment of a slightly higher price to the new supplier.

The equivalent annual percentage cost of losing cash discounts by delaying payment to those suppliers who offer a discount must always be very carefully weighed in the balance. Here we have the counterpart to the arguments recited above concerning discounts offered to customers. Loss of cash discount from suppliers by delaying payment to them could represent a very high price to pay for what is effectively a source of cash inflow.

There is, of course, a natural delay between the time a check is signed and the time it is charged against the bank account of the person signing it. This delay is a function of the efficiency of the postal service, the efficiency with which the recipient pays checks into his bank, the efficiency of the banking system for clearing checks, and interruptions by weekends and holidays. This delay could be of considerable value to a firm's cash flow and unless there are strong reasons for so doing, it seems senseless to short circuit this leisurely process, for example by the use of first class mail or direct bank transfers when settling suppliers' accounts.

The amount payable to suppliers is of course determined not only by credit terms but also by the level of purchases. Clearly this line on the cash forecast will be largely affected by decisions as to the volume of production, the level of inventories, and the frequency of ordering or delivery of purchased items.

Line 7 *Wages, salaries, and labor-related expenses*—Because there is little or no room for maneuver as to the time of settlement of these items, only volume-related, scale-related, and once-off or one-time actions can normally have any impact. However the selection of a production policy for meeting seasonal peaks in demand will have its impact upon the pattern of wage payments. Clearly, a policy that maintains a constant level of production (allowing inventory to act as a buffer) will create a different pattern of wage cash flow than a policy that allows production levels to vary in harmony with peaks and troughs in demand.

Lines 8 and 9 *Other payments*—There is again little room for maneuver here. Clearly the maximum allowable amount of credit should be taken.

Line 10 *Taxes*—Taxes are due and payable on a date or dates determined by law and so once again there is little room to maneuver. However the legal determination of the latest date of payment is worthy of careful study in case there is opportunity for so arranging the firm's affairs as to qualify for the maximum legal period of credit. See for example the comments made below regarding the impact that the dividend decision might have on the legal date for payment of United Kingdom Corporation Tax (the tax on corporate profits).

The annual payment of taxes on corporate profits could represent a significant transfer of funds from the firm's bank account. Indeed for a profitable concern it could represent in any year the largest amount for which a single check is drawn. If this is the case, it will no doubt pay to make special arrangements with the bank for clearing the check in order to ensure that the precise impact on cash flow is determined to the day, thereby not only controlling cash flow but also ensuring that any loss of interest receivable or increase in interest payable is kept to a minimum.

Line 11 *Purchase of buildings, plant, equipment*—Here is an item where there is considerable scope for management control. The capital investment decision itself clearly has its impact upon cash flow—for example, management must choose with particular care the date on which each project shall start. Similarly the chosen nature of the project itself will affect cash flows—for example, whether a labor or capital intensive route is selected. However, let us consider aspects of cash flow beyond the capital investment decision itself. Alternative methods of payment are normally available and should be considered. Deferred payment terms might be negotiated instead of outright purchase; installment or hire purchase terms may be available; leasing might be considered as an alternative to ownership. In all of these cases the true cost of so delaying cash outflows must be very carefully computed so that an unnecessarily expensive route is not inadvertently chosen. This is a similar consideration to that which should be applied to management's decision to delay payment to suppliers on forfeiture of cash discounts.

Lines 12 and 13 *Interest and dividend payments, capital repayments*—Here we move into that area of cash flow described in an earlier chapter as financial obligations. Payment of interest on and repayment of borrowed money are contractual liabilities and default can have dire consequences for the firm; payment of a preference, or preferred, dividend is contractual in the United Kingdom (although not so in the U.S.A.) unless profits are inadequate to cover such dividends when they typically accumulate and will be paid when profits improve. In the United States, there are cumulative and non-cumulative preferred stocks. With non-cumulative preferred stock, if dividends are not paid for a particular period, they will not be paid at all. Payment of ordinary, or equity, or common dividend is more a moral than a contractual obligation but, if shareholders' expectations as to dividend are not fulfilled, this could result in an adverse effect upon the market value of such shares. For all these reasons, there would seem to be little scope for maneuver by management other than determining the amount of ordinary, equity, or common dividend. However this is not strictly true, because initially there is considerable scope for management control through determination of dates of payment. For example, it would seem senseless to select a date for payment of interest or dividend that coincides with a period of peak seasonal inventory (which normally implies high negative cash flow) or with the date of payment of tax on corporate profits.

For administrative convenience, it is common to move sufficient cash into a special bank account against which interest and/or dividend checks shall be charged as and when presented. As was the case with the tax payment, management once again has the need for making special arrangements with the bank as to the precise date on which funds shall be made available to meet the interest or dividend payment. However, as was the case with payment to suppliers, here again there is a natural delay between the time the check is signed and the time it is charged against the special bank account. For this reason management has the opportunity for fine tuning of the period of time over which funds need to be made available to meet the payment of interest and dividend.

The relationship in the UK between the payment of a dividend and the acceleration of the payment of tax on corporate profits—ACT or Advanced Corporation Tax—was discussed in Chapter 3. Briefly, if a dividend is paid, a substantial advance payment on account of the next annual payment of tax on corporate profits falls due for payment; the amount of the payment bears a direct relationship to the amount of dividend paid. Therefore, under current United Kingdom tax legislation, the dividend decision *not only* affects cash flow through the dividend itself, *but also* through the associated acceleration in the payment of tax on corporate profits. For this reason the use of a non-cash dividend, i.e. scrip, or stock, dividend, commends itself *but also* delays cash outflow on taxation. Many UK public companies have done this: for example Guest, Keen & Nettlefolds in 1974 offered its Ordinary shareholders the opportunity of taking shares in lieu of a cash dividend and relevant extracts from the letter circulated to shareholders are reproduced in Figure 4.3. Unfortunately for other public companies, a change in United Kingdom tax legislation in 1975 imposed Advance Corporation Tax payment on scrip dividends also.

Figure 4.3 Extract from a letter to the Ordinary shareholders of Guest Keen and Nettle-folds Limited from Chairman Raymond Brooks, dated October 22, 1974

```
'... the Directors proposed that the shareholders be given the opportunity
to elect to receive fully paid Ordinary shares in the Company in return for
giving up the right to receive...the interim dividend for 1974.

'... To the extent that shareholders elect to receive Ordinary shares, funds
are retained for use in the business, leading to a reduction in cash outflow.
Depending on the number of shares in respect of which the election is made,
there could be a substantial saving of cash to the Company, which is especially
valuable at the present time.

'... The Company would also benefit in that, as a result of the scheme, there
would be a deferment of tax corresponding to the Advance Corporation Tax on
the dividend which would otherwise have to be paid.

'... If all shareholders elected to receive shares instead of interim dividend,
there would be a saving to the Company of the whole of the amount of the
dividend, £3,904,915, and the Advance Corporation Tax of £1,923,316 would not
be payable.'
```

Line 19 *Cash and bank balances at the end of current month*—This line reveals the cumulative net effect of all cash inflows and outflows each month. When one considers the examples of management action which have been suggested above in considering many of the items making up this amount, it becomes clear that there is ample scope for management to restructure the pattern of future cash flows so as to minimize the extent of a potential cash deficit or to react to an ongoing situation which appears to be getting out of hand. When all possible action has been considered this line will reveal whether a deficit remains. Only now, in the knowledge that this is the most favorable adverse position, will management begin its search for additional finance from outside the firm. Full consideration of the various sources that might be available is presented in a later chapter.

4.6 DIRECTING MANAGEMENT EFFORT

When seeking either to improve the plan or to correct the ongoing cash position, to what extent should management get involved in detail? A line has to be drawn somewhere if only because time is too short to permit a detailed examination of every single item of cash flow. A similar problem presents itself when preparing the cash forecast and again when analyzing the actual position as a basis for presenting control information. There is never enough time to examine everything. Unfortunately, time is always short so people must constantly strive to make the most of whatever time is made available. But where shall the line be drawn in paying attention to detail? The answer generally is to pay greatest attention to the few significant items which command the greatest proportion of value and to pay progressively less attention to the many trivial items which command an insignificant proportion of total value and hence where the payoff, if any, in terms of significant benefits to be gained must be relatively small. The basic relationship between the significant few and the trivial many is enshrined in the well known Pareto Curve (so named after the Italian social theorist who, in the nineteenth century, observed and first wrote up the phenomenon) sometimes referred to as the 80/20 Rule or ABC Analysis.

If the composition of any group of like items is examined (for example a firm's customers, suppliers, product range, inventory, cash inflows, cash outflows) it will almost always be found that there are relatively few large value items but many small value items. In fact, if all the items in any group are ranged in descending order of value, the top 20 percent by volume of the items may well account for as much as 80 percent of the total value represented by the group: hence the title 80/20 Rule. The grossly oversimplified example in Figure 4.4 demonstrates the principle. Notice that if all customers had an equal value of sales, the line on the graph at the bottom left would be a straight diagonal line—instead the familiar Pareto Curve emerges; notice also that the top

Number of customers	Value of sales, $	Cumulative number of customers	Cumulative value of sales, $	Cumulative percentage of customers, %	Cumulative percentage of sales, %
10 largest in terms of sales value	1000	10	1000	12,5	50.0
Next 10	600	20	1600	25.0	80.0
Next 10	150	30	1750	37.5	87.5
Next 10	100	40	1850	50.0	92.5
Next 10	60	50	1910	62.5	95.5
Next 10	40	60	1950	75.0	97.5
Next 10	30	70	1980	87.5	99.0
10 smallest in terms of sales value	20	80	2000	100.0	100.0

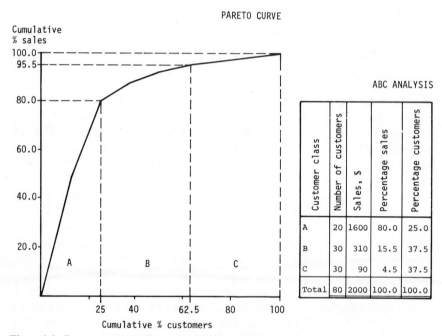

Figure 4.4 Demonstration of Pareto (or 80/20 or ABC) analysis of sales to customers

25 percent of customers accounts for 80 percent of the sales—not quite 80/20;
notice also that the most significant return for effort can only come from this
25 percent (class A)—the classes B and C must return progressively poorer value
per unit of effort put in.

Thus management effort should always be directed to the front end of the
Pareto Curve—the significant few, the class A items. In terms of human en-
deavor—be it managerial, administrative, or clerical—it takes just as much effort
to deal with an item at the front end of the Pareto Curve as it does to deal with

108

an item at the back end. Therefore, beware of squandering continuing effort over the class C items in any group which represent the back end of that group's Pareto Curve where the payoff must be insignificant. Redirect that effort to the class A items at the front end of the Pareto Curve for the next group of items. Herein lies the successful orientation for either forecasting, monitoring, or controlling cash flow.

4.7 SIGNIFICANCE OF WORKING CAPITAL

Any consideration of the control of cash flow or direction of management effort must at some stage consider the role of working capital because it is here that much cash can get tied down. In theory, working capital (that is, current assets minus current liabilities) represents the rapid circulation of funds beginning with receipt of materials into inventory, its progression through work-in-progress into finished goods, dispatch or shipment to the customer, the collection from the customer of cash in settlement which is used to purchase more material, and so on round and round. However, working capital does not always circulate quickly and smoothly. Unfortunately, it may slow down and grow unnecessarily large, thereby sucking valuable cash resources into unremunerative backwaters or worse still into whirlpools from which it might never emerge. Much can be done to control cash by efficient management of working capital, be it represented by inventories, debtors (or receivables), creditors (or payables), or cash itself. These elements each represent vast areas of study in themselves and, therefore, a detailed consideration is beyond the scope of this book. However, let us conclude this chapter by a very brief overview of action which might be taken to improve control over these elements of working capital. In each case the watchword must be "keep working capital moving." Bear in mind also that any reduction in working capital has a dual benefit in that there is also a saving in those costs, e.g. interest and handling, that would be avoided if the working capital were not carried.

4.8 CONTROL OF INVENTORIES

The impact on cash flow of improved inventory control can be appreciated by reflection upon the cash tank analogy (see Figure 2.4). A build-up of inventories in effect opens up the control valve on one of the outlet pipes. Conversely a reduction has the practical effect of opening up the control valve on one of the inlet pipes. Ineffective control of inventories could amount almost to an unconscious opening of an outlet valve or worse still could represent a corroded hole in the cash tank out of which the valuable liquid slowly but continuously escapes.

What is included in inventory and where does the value lie? Inventory does not represent only stocks of raw materials and finished goods, but also every "holding" stage between raw material delivery and final acceptance by the customer. In other words, it also embraces work-in-progress, sub-assemblies, finished goods in transit, consignment goods on sale or return, and also non-production inventories such as consumables, maintenance materials, fuel, packing materials, stationery and stocks of other administration, selling and distribution supplies. Frequently, the grand total represents the largest single item in that part of the balance sheet which reveals the way in which capital is deployed about the business, i.e. it is often larger in amount than fixed assets. For this reason there is often considerable scope for saving and thus for liberating excessive amounts of cash tied up. We have seen that there is a wide range of items embraced within inventories and, therefore, there is need for selectivity when applying management effort. For this reason, an application of the 80/20 Rule, or ABC Analysis, discussed earlier in this chapter will have the most significant impact upon cash flow through the concentration of management effort on those significant items at the front end of the Pareto Curve. Furthermore, it must be realized that more cash becomes progressively tied up in an item as it progresses through from raw materials to finished goods. This is particularly significant to a vertically integrated firm organized on divisional lines. An indiscriminate instruction to "get down the level of inventories" is an open invitation to divisions to complete their part of the work and push out their inventory to the next division down the line nearer to the finished state. In this case, all that has happened is that more cash has been pumped into inventory as it moves down the chain. The stage of completion at which they are held clearly has a critical impact on the total cash tied up in inventories.

The unattainable Utopian goal is to have zero inventories but clearly this is impossible. In theory, we must carry inventory to smooth out any imbalance in production/marketing effort, to ensure that all reasonable demands can be met as expeditiously as possible, and to provide an insurance, or hedge, against failure in delivery or escalation of delivery price. Naturally, this theory applies in practice also. But are the inventory levels down to the minimum necessary to achieve these theoretical goals? Over and above this minimum, how much inventory results from bad provisioning, an over-cautious attitude to the risk of being out-of-stock, the residue left in the wake of design modifications and other changes of plan or simply just "what is left over from production"? Perhaps the attitude towards customer service is an over-generous one: the amount of finished goods that must be carried to ensure 100 percent customer satisfaction could be crippling—a considerable liberation of cash might be achieved by acceptance of something less than 100 percent service cover. Much has been written on the need for careful predetermination of inventory levels and various techniques involving different degrees of mathematical sophistication are recommended from time to time. Arguments as to their practical applicability and utility roll back and forth. However four points are worthy of mention:

1 Minimum safety levels *must* be fixed and moreover they must be determined by a responsible manager at a fairly senior level bearing in mind that such levels, once fixed, will commit cash to inventory more or less permanently. This is the critical implication of inventory safety levels. If the minimum levels are determined at a less senior level, say by a warehouse supervisor, there is a risk that such levels may be fixed by him with the most critical implication being whether or not he might run out of stock rather than whether the firm can afford to commit cash in this way. After all, the warehouse supervisor will no doubt feel that he has done a good job if he never runs out of stock. Herein lies an open invitation to overstock for safety.

2 The total amount of inventory held at any one time is a function of the minimum safety stock plus a fluctuating amount determined by the relationship between the delivered quantity and the demand or take-off. Hence the higher the delivered quantity, the higher must be the average overall inventory level and the greater the amount of cash thereby tied up. This is demonstrated in the simple sequence of examples A, B, and C in Figure 4.5 which demonstrates that, for the same level of demand, an average inventory level of either 170 or 70 or 45 can be determined by variations in delivered quantities. Thus, the essential levels which should be determined in addition to minimum safety levels are delivered quantities, or production batch sizes, as the case may be.

3 A further determinant of the total inventory volume is the number of locations at which minimum levels are held. Clearly the lowest overall inventory level is achieved if only one central pool is maintained. On the other hand, there are a number of very good practical reasons which demand a degree of duplication. However, such duplication must be kept to the minimum consistent with efficient, economical production and sales activity. This should be the decision of a fairly senior level of management. Beware the multiplicity of self-help or do-it-yourself pools which individuals salt away like squirrels pending the proverbial rainy day!

4 Another aspect of duplication that causes an unnecessary amount of cash to be tied up in inventory is the uncontrolled extension of the range of items carried. The number of items held in stock should be periodically reviewed to establish whether it is possible to reduce the range by the application of variety reduction or by standardization of materials, components, or stores. Moreover, if it is possible to weed out the range in this way, any redundant items should

Example A: safety stock 20, monthly demand 50, delivered quantity 300. Note maximum level = 320, average level = 170, i.e. 20 + (300/2)

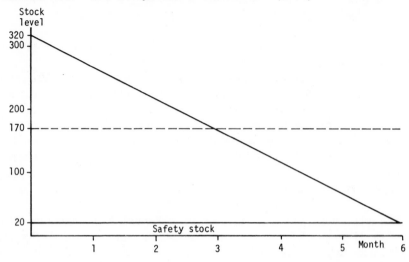

Example B: safety stock 20, monthly demand 50, delivered quantity 100. Note maximum level = 120, average level = 70, i.e. 20 + (100/2)

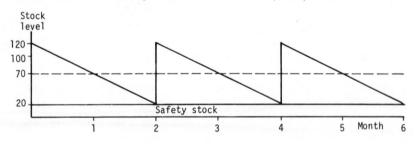

Example C: safety stock 20, monthly demand 50, delivered quantity 50. Note maximum level = 65, average level = 45, i.e. 20 + (50/2)

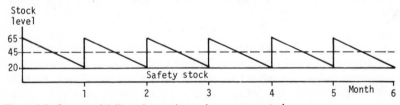

Figure 4.5 Impact of delivered quantity on inventory control

be converted into cash as expeditiously as possible in order to prevent their adding to the length of tail of the Pareto curve.

Of course, one must not overlook the possibility that cash committed to inventory may be a good investment in the light of potential "windfall profits" which can be earned by avoiding future price escalations. This is particularly significant at times of rapid inflation. While this is true, such commitments of cash should be very carefully evaluated against both the costs of providing the parcel of cash which is thereby tied up and also any other additional out-of-pocket costs incurred in laying down and keeping the additional inventory. It must also be carefully weighed against the possibility of a price *decrease*.

Information on movements in inventory levels is necessary if management is to have sufficient warning of the need for action to conserve cash flow. For this reason, such information is incorporated into the suggested monthly liquidity report shown previously in Figure 4.1.

4.9 CREDIT MANAGEMENT

As was the case with the control of inventories, reference to our cash tank in Figure 2.4 will also reveal the impact upon cash flow of improved control of debtors or receivables. Delay in collection from customers is equivalent to an outflow of cash while improvement in the speed of collection creates an inflow of cash. The area of management responsibility which is labelled "credit control" (or "credit management") traditionally relates to the prompt collection of amounts owed by customers; however when considering the total impact upon cash flow one must be aware of the total area for control. As was stressed earlier in this chapter when discussing collections from customers, this area begins with acceptance of goods by the customer, i.e. the termination point in inventory, and ends with the banking of the check or cash in payment. Thus, the total area of control of debtors or receivables must embrace the following three stages of control:

1 Prompt presentation of invoices and other demands for payment.

2 Control of credit taken by customers.

3 Prompt banking of collections.

Control of credit taken by customers is of course the meat of the exercise: if only sales could be for cash what considerable economies in cash flow could be achieved! But extension of credit must be accepted as part of normal trading and, because it is a most powerful means of increasing sales volume, it represents a very valuable element in the total marketing package. However, it also represents a considerable risk to the continuing existence of the firm because no firm can live long without any collections from customers. Moreover, not only does customer credit affect cash flow, it has a clear impact upon profitability. For example, if a profit margin of 8 percent is earned on sales at a time when annual interest rates are 16 percent, then failure to collect within six months effectively eliminates that profit; furthermore, failure to collect at all represents a bad debt dead loss of $92 per $100 sales not collected and this robs the 8 percent profit margin from the next $1250 of sales also. The most important contribution which credit management can make to cash control lies in directing marketing effort into those channels which represent good credit risks rather than in trying to extract collections from those customers which the firm should never have become involved with in the first place. Thus, credit control, or credit management, must be seen as a positive rather than a negative function. Effectively applied it will both increase sales volume (by the extension of credit) and enhance cash flow (by the control of credit). The scope of credit management is itself quite wide, embracing as it does the following:

1 Checking and advising on the credit rating of potential new customers through the various sources of credit information that are available to the diligent credit manager, e.g. surveys produced by professional credit reporting agencies such as Dun & Bradstreet, trade and personal references, and face-to-face discussions with and investigation of prospective customers.

2 Monitoring and reporting on the continuing credit rating of existing customers.

3 Arranging for credit insurance where this is considered to be desirable. (With overseas customers this is often thought to be more economically justifiable than with domestic customers due to the longer credit terms which frequently have to be offered and to the possibility of political risks over and above the normal commercial risk of a bad debt.)

4 Following up slow payers and attempting to ensure that all customers adhere to their agreed credit terms.

Credit management appears to be much further developed in North America than it is in the United Kingdom, perhaps due historically to the greater distances involved and the different attitudes towards branch banking.

How much effort is it worth putting into credit management and particularly into collections? Without a doubt, the application of ABC Analysis or the

Pareto Curve will pay rich dividends here. One credit manager found that 60 percent of each month's cash collections came from only five customers. These were designated "key accounts" and were given individual attention in order to identify and clear up invoice queries at the earliest possible date and to ensure that collections were made as efficiently as possible. These key accounts at the front end of the Pareto Curve adequately justify such personal service. Customers outside the key accounts were covered by telephone or personal visit but if the outstanding balance was below $500 they were dealt with on a collection letter basis unless they were considerably overdue. Clearly very different attitudes were adopted towards home and export customers.

Two relatively simple means of accelerating collections are by offering discounts to customers or by factoring, i.e. selling, the debts to a finance house specializing in this service. However, in each case the cost of acceleration should be very carefully computed and compared to the cost of alternative sources of cash inflow. The true cost of offering discounts to customers for prompt payment is to be found by relating the amount of the discount to the number of days or months acceleration in payment and converting to an annual percentage. This was demonstrated earlier in this chapter when discussing collections from customers. Simple calculations reveal that a 2½ percent discount offered to accelerate collections by two months is equivalent to paying 15 percent per year for the benefit of this source of cash inflow. The true cost of factoring should be calculated on a similar basis but the arithmetic is slightly more complicated in that the factoring company might also be providing certain administrative services as part of the package. The total cost of factoring is not always purely one of financing accelerated cash flows.

Information on the current status of collections from customers is necessary if management is to have sufficient warning of the need for action. For this reason such information is incorporated into the suggested monthly liquidity report which was reproduced as part of Figure 4.1.

4.10 INVENTORY AND CREDIT MANAGEMENT

In Sections 4.8 and 4.9 we have looked at the control of inventories and the control of collections from customers as two isolated studies. This frequently is the case in practice also: different functional areas of management are responsible for inventory and for credit management, each area working diligently yet independently towards achievement of its own goals. But could it just be possible that these goals might occasionally be inconsistent? Bearing in mind that both credit and inventory are part of the service given to customers and reflected in the price charged to the customer, it is surprising that these two functions are not more frequently brought under one common control to ensure consistency of policy and, above all, economy in the amount of cash locked up jointly between the two functions.

A simple example of potential inconsistency arises where, in order to assist cash flow, inventory is disposed of at an attractive price to the customer. This certainly might have the desired effect of reducing the level of inventories but if the amount involved simply moves through into debtors, or receivables, where it lies for an extended period of time, perhaps the potential cash flow from inventory reduction might not be realized any earlier than it would have been without the special offer. In this example, the only effect of the exercise is a reduction in profits due to the price concession given to the customer. Clearly a price concession to encourage the movement of inventory is only of real value if it is married to special (shorter) credit terms within a complete customer package deal.

We have already observed that the average level of inventory is a function of minimum safety level, delivered quantity and demand or take-off. This, of course, applies to both supplier and customer. It is not beyond the bounds of possibility that the combined level of inventory carried by both supplier and customer exceeds their combined needs. Perhaps closer cooperation between supplier and customer could result in a modification of production/delivery schedules to the mutual advantage of both parties. Moreover any change in the take-off rate by the customer could be accommodated by an adjustment to his credit terms and still provide net advantage to both parties. The advantage could be through cost saving, improved cash flow, or both. Whereas it takes exactly the same amount of cash to finance $100 of inventory as it does to finance $100 of debtors or receivables, the costs and risks associated with the carrying of each are quite different. So again there could be an advantage in negotiating a complete inventory/delivery/price/credit package with the customer.

4.11   CONTROL OF CASH

This chapter has been concerned with the management and control of cash flows and recent sections have looked more specifically into certain aspects of working capital control. An earlier section contained a number of references to the need to control carefully the precise timing of certain significant cash outflows. However there is no merit in controlling cash flows if cash itself is not also controlled. Moreover, cash represents a further element of working capital and for this reason alone requires control. Let us think of 'cash' in this current context very broadly as cash balances, bank balances, short-term deposits and other near cash items.

It is necessary to maintain certain cash balances or at least to have ready access to cash in order to meet normal demands on a day-to-day basis. Clearly a firm needs to be able to pay its employees at the end of each week or month. Moreover many firms prefer to maintain an additional amount, over and above normal needs, as a contingency reserve to be called upon only in times of unexpected financial strain (we shall return to this in a later chapter). But is the total cash held throughout the firm in excess of reasonable requirements? We spoke above about the need to keep inventory levels at a minimum—are cash and near cash balances at a minimum also or is an excessive amount tied up which could be redeployed more effectively throughout the firm? In assessing the adequacy of total cash balances, management ought to take into consideration the following items:

1 Cash or checks collected from customers by travelling salesmen but not yet deposited in the bank. Is this process as efficient as possible?

2 Cash or checks in transit between different locations, e.g. between branches and head office. Is this process as efficient as possible?

3 Cash and bank balances of whatever amount, for whatever purpose, and wherever held. Is there unnecessary duplication of cash floats, advances, reserves, and the like which would represent a significantly lower total if centrally held or if replenished by smaller amounts at more frequent intervals? (Similar principles apply as to determination of inventory levels.) If there are several bank accounts, do some have unfavorable balances while some have favorable balances, thus incurring unnecessarily high interest charges?

4 Short-term deposits and investments. Is the amount justifiable and is its rate of return appropriate to its ease of liquidation?

Instantaneous transfer or offsetting of balances through the British branch banking system helps considerably to minimize uneconomical disposition of funds. On the other hand, in North America there are spectacular benefits to be earned by the more efficient *physical* transfer of cash or near cash items from one location to another. One American airline corporation effected considerable economy in its total cash balances by the simple expedient of flying cash and checks back to a central location by its own aircraft on a daily basis. On the other hand, a British company need simply make arrangements with its bank that all balances on all its local bank accounts throughout the United Kingdom are automatically cleared daily to one central account.

The counter-productive nature of duplication of cash balances must not be underestimated. For this reason, it is important that management try to avoid getting itself into the position where it is *unable* to remedy such a situation. This is particularly important where business is carried on in different countries, some of which operate restrictions on the free transferability of cash. In such circumstances, management, by all means legally available, must try to avoid the accumulation of cash in countries that impose such restrictions. It is known that some multinational corporations have excess cash balances immobilized in one country while borrowing expensively in another.

Finally, in our consideration of the control of cash let us not forget that it is a commodity that possesses intrinsic value of itself on an international scale and as such needs to be deployed to maximize this value. More efficient deployment must consider the impact of changing international interest rates, currency exchange rate fluctuations, and international rates of inflation. Little wonder that in larger firms the management of cash can be a well justified full-time job in its own right.

Wenman Plastics:
Part 4

Before reading this part of the case study, readers are first invited to review the earlier parts of the case and in particular their answers to Question 1 (Part 1) and Question 5 (Part 3).

Claude and Karl Wenman agreed to get together quite early next Sunday morning so that they would not be interrupted by the normal everyday problems of their business. In this way they would be able to devote their undivided attention to the problem that was presented by Claude's forecast of cash requirements over the forthcoming year to March 1974 and reproduced as Exhibit 6. Whereas Claude felt reasonably confident that it would be possible to raise the necessary money, he wished to review the situation with his father to see if it would be possible to reduce the required amount without creating undue damage either to sales or to profit. In anticipation of the meeting, Claude sat down to review the decisions that had been taken regarding the development of Wenman Plastics' future business (as set down in numbered sections in Part 1 of this case study) and made the following notes to form a framework for discussion with his father on Sunday morning (the numbered sections correspond to those used in Part 1).

1 Market Policy Generally

a The decision to make a broad scale introduction has determined the speed with which necessary facilities and working capital must be made available. This is reflected in the pattern of additional financing revealed by Exhibit 6. No doubt a less ambitious start followed by a more gradual build up would reduce the demand for cash by spreading out the need for facilities and working capital requirements. On the other hand, Claude feels that a less ambitious start is not desirable as it might not create an adequate impact on the market.

b Perhaps the decision to introduce two products has had a particularly severe impact on cash flow. On the one hand the modular bathroom accessories will require the provision of considerable working capital to finance the inventory which the product range and color choice imply; moreover the distribution through hardware stores and builders' merchants dictates a wide spread of accounts receivable which, if control is not careful, could begin to extend their period of customer credit. On the other hand the special purpose plastic packaging will be made to customer specification which would result in lower inventory per dollar of sales; moreover there will no doubt be fewer customers which should ease the problem of control. The bathroom accessories product is, therefore, likely to have a much greater adverse impact upon cash flow than is the special purpose plastic packaging. But Claude feels that the launch of both products is necessary to maintain credibility in the market and also to make optimum use of production facilities.

2 Market Potential

a The cash forecast reproduced as Exhibit 6 has been produced on the assumption of rapid achievement of an annual sales level of $6 million. A different rate of takeoff through the achievement of sales of either a higher *or* a lower annual rate than this will affect the need for cash because the levels of inventories, debtors or accounts receivable, creditors or accounts payable and, of course, potential cash flow from operations will all be different.

b Similarly, the cash position must change if a different seasonal pattern is experienced to that anticipated, again due mainly to the change that will occur in inventories and accounts receivable. However, Claude accepts that this is just one of the risks that must be faced.

3 Facilities

a It is fortunate that not only are premises available for rent (the need to build or to purchase would have quite a different impact upon cash flow) but also all necessary services are provided and therefore no cash is required for their provision.

b Fixed asset purchases are a critical feature in determining the cash position. Three factors have helped determine the $1 million estimate that has been made:

1. The decision to operate two shifts determines the volume of equipment required.

2. The decision to purchase new rather than secondhand equipment (if available) has determined the amount required.

3. The cash flow position could be eased if either leasing is considered rather than purchase or if deferred payment terms can be arranged for some or all of the items of equipment.

4 Production Policy

a The decision to produce at a steady level will cause inventories to build up to a peak (reflected by a drain on cash) in the months preceding peak sales. Perhaps a different production policy will have a more favorable impact upon cash flow. On the other hand, a steady production policy has always been followed in the past and is much easier to control.

b If there is any delay or major obstacle in obtaining and training staff or in getting the new plant on stream, the requirement for cash will change.

5 Inventory Policy

a The following decisions have been taken regarding inventory levels:

1. Raw materials: two months normal production requirement.

2. Work-in-progress: two weeks normal production.

3. Finished goods: two months average sales demand.

These decisions have a clear impact upon both the amount and pattern of cash requirement. Acceptance of lower levels will ease cash flow but, on the other hand, will add a greater dimension of risk to the operation than Claude wishes to accept.

b It has been decided to offer the new range of modular bathroom accessories in five colors. Inventory must be carried for each of these colors. If the sales mix gets out of balance, the inventories will similarly get out of balance and thereby increase in total and will create an even greater drain on cash.

6 Income and Expenditure

a Whereas the items are only estimates and may themselves turn out to be incorrect, it is possible that even if these estimates are correct as to amount, the estimate as to their timing (set up in Exhibit 4) may be incorrect. In this case, the pattern of cash flow will be affected.

b On the other hand, the possibility of consciously changing the timing of the major items must be actively considered.

7 Financing

a1 Exhibit 6 has been produced on the assumption of monthly credit from suppliers. If it were possible to negotiate extended credit terms with major supplier(s), the cash position would be eased through the delay in cash outflow.

a2 On the other hand, if customers (particularly the new ones) press for, or take extended credit, the cash position will be considerably worsened.

a3 It has been decided *not* to offer cash discounts to customers for prompt settlement. October and November represent months of peak cash deficit due in part to the need to await collection from high sales in September and October following the seasonal low in August. Perhaps it might be worth offering a cash discount on sales in October provided this did not set an expensive precedent for the rest of the year.

b Father's reluctance to offer for sale additional shares restricts the availability of additional finance.

c1 His insistence on maintenance of the 20 percent dividend not only causes an outflow of cash on the payment of dividend but it also accelerates the outflow of cash on taxes due to the liability for Advance Corporation Tax set up by the dividend payment.

c2 The dates chosen for the half yearly dividend payment are particularly unfortunate as October is the month of peak cash deficit. June and December would represent a much better choice of payment dates.

d The availability of short-term investments is helpful but the decision to cash these in April denies the availability of a contingency reserve in case of need at a later date.

e Fortunately, tne existing premises provide the basis for a secured loan and moreover there is no requirement for repayment by annual installments. The cash position would be further improved by negotiation of a complete sale and lease back agreement but this would entail losing control of the premises which have been in the family since 1962.

Claude realized that, irrespective of the decisions taken with his father at their meeting on Sunday morning, Wenman Plastics would almost certainly require additional financing during the year ended March 1974. Furthermore, he realized that he ought to get a clearer indication of the length of time for which he might require such financing beyond the end of March 1974. Therefore, he wondered whether it might be a good idea to attempt to project his cash flow position beyond March 1974. It could be that his father's decision on the issue of additional share capital might have to be reconsidered. So Claude sat up late into the night to turn his thoughts to a longer term forecast of cash requirements for Wenman Plastics Limited.

Question 7

Should the longer-term cash forecast for Wenman Plastics Ltd. adopt the same format as that employed in Exhibit 6? How much detail is required in the longer-term forecast? How far ahead should it look?

Long-Term
Cash Forecasts

*Up to now we have concentrated our attention
on forecasting and controlling cash flow
in the short term—an essential exercise
if management is to ensure that the firm
is able to pay its way and so stay in business
in the near future. However, there is an additional need
to forecast cash flow in the longer term.
The need here is quite different from
the short-term need: it is to test the viability
of alternative future courses of action
and to ensure adequate funds to meet future requirements
for cash created by the selected alternative.
In this chapter, we therefore turn our attention
to the content, format, and frequency
of the long-term cash forecast.*

5.1 COMPARISON WITH SHORT-TERM FORECASTING

In Chapter 3 we focused our attention on the short-term cash forecast. The object of that particular exercise was to guide appropriate and timely management action towards improved control of cash flow. In Chapter 4 we looked at some of the actions that management is able to take when exercising such control. Thus, the short-term cash forecast is directed towards tactical control of an ongoing situation and typically will look ahead several months.

But the availability of cash, in the right amounts and at the right time, is more than just a short-term matter. The future existence of the firm depends upon the continuing availability of cash flow to meet the firm's needs as it develops and grows. In addition to the forecasting of cash flows in the short term, there is thus the need to forecast cash flows in the long term if the firm is at least to continue in existence as a viable economic unit within the longer-term planning period. Future development and growth depend upon operational actions and plans, but these can be to no avail if the firm runs out of cash en route. Thus, the long-term cash forecast is concerned with the evaluation of future *strategic* courses of action, which is somewhat different from the tactical orientation of short-term cash forecasting.

The long-term cash forecast will typically look ahead several years. Its objectives are to ascertain the financial consequences of future operational plans and to assist in the selection of that long-term pattern of financing which must be developed in order to achieve those long-term operational plans which have been selected. However, the long- and short-term cash forecasts are inter-related in two ways:

1 The long-term forecast reflects plans that will, in effect, act as both determinants of and constraints upon the short-term position.

2 The short-term forecast will initially provide month by month detail for the first year of the long-term forecast.

5.2 RELATIONSHIP TO CORPORATE PLANNING

We have seen that the long-term cash forecast is concerned with ensuring continued economic viability of the firm within the forthcoming planning period. We have also seen that the long-term cash forecast will reveal how much financing is required to carry through those long-term courses of action which management has selected. For these reasons, it is clear that long-term cash forecasting is inextricably bound up with the firm's long-term operational corporate or strategic plan; it would be pointless to attempt producing a long-term cash forecast as an isolated exercise. A corporate or strategic plan first attempts to review both the firm's current strengths and weaknesses and the anticipated future opportunities and threats in the economic and market environment in which it will operate. It then selects that strategy, or course of action, which should ensure that the firm has a better chance of economic survival as the future unfolds: forewarned is forearmed!

The major elements of the strategy will be operational but it is also necessary to select a financial strategy. Generally, this will simply reflect and evaluate the operational elements, but occasions could arise when the financial strategy might not reflect but, in fact, be in conflict with the operational strategy. We will return to this possibility later because of its importance. Should it arise, management must decide which element of the strategy shall have priority—the operational or the financial. However let us first consider the mechanics of compiling the long-term cash forecast.

'. . .there is little merit in attempting to plan
ahead any further than is practically desirable
and necessary. . .'

5.3 "HOW LONG IS LONG?"

This is a question that is frequently asked of any long-term planning exercise.
Moreover it is a very important question, bearing in mind the difficulties and
uncertainties that surround forecasting. As the planning horizon is pushed
farther into the future, the quality of any plan must degenerate because the
individual forecasts that comprise the plan become progressively less reliable.
There is little merit, therefore, in attempting to plan ahead any further than is
practically desirable or necessary. But "How long is desirable?" is not the easiest
question to answer either! Selection of an appropriate long-term planning horizon for any firm is a matter which must be peculiar to that firm, having taken
account of the nature of its business and the environment in which it operates.
For example, a company whose business consists of planting forests in order to
grow trees as a basis for producing timber which it then pulps and converts into
paper from which it produces paper products through its own mills must, of
practical necessity, select a longer planning horizon than a company involved in
retailing fashion wear through a boutique operated from rented premises in the
local shopping center.

However, although it is not possible to answer precisely "How long is long," the following is a short list of factors that will be considered when determining the planning horizon in any specific case:

1   The throughput time required to complete one cycle from initial contact with the customer, through the purchasing and production process, to successful conclusion with that customer. In certain industries—for example, a civil engineering firm involved with the construction of a hydroelectric dam—this cycle time is quite lengthy, and would therefore seem to indicate the necessity for a longer planning horizon than might otherwise be required. One well known contractor changed its planning horizon from four to twelve years for this reason.

2   The estimated life of the products currently being sold. A firm must consider its continued existence in the light of its need to find replacement products— the longer the product life, the further ahead the plan must extend.

3   Similarly, the length of time required to develop a new product is a critical factor. If a product has a six year lead time from initial development to coming onstream, it would seem pointless to plan ahead only three years.

4   The speed of change and rate of obsolescence in those major technologies which impinge upon the firm's operations must also have their impact on how far ahead the firm must plan if it is to initiate appropriate anticipatory action.

5   The existence of ongoing financial obligations. For example, any significant forthcoming repayments of capital could help to determine the planning horizon if only to ensure that the firm is able to meet its obligations and to continue safely in business after having met them.

6   The general degree of flexibility of the firm, i.e. how quickly the firm is able to change course. The longer it takes, the further ahead the planning horizon must be. This factor is often closely related to the degree of intensity of capital investment. Generally speaking, the more capital-intensive the firm becomes, the more difficult it is to change its product orientation. For example, once the Ford Motor Company has laid down an automobile assembly line, it cannot quickly change it over to the brewing of beer or even to the manufacture of electric washing machines.

Several of these factors may be present simultaneously and some may indicate the need for a longer planning horizon than others. For this reason the length chosen is frequently a compromise. (A former Director of Planning at IBM has been reported as stating: "We chose five years because four years are too short and six years are too long.") Frequently, in practice, the attitude to planning differs over the complete span of the planning period. For example, the degree of detail might decline as planning pushes further into the future (fairly detailed plans for three years and a general outline only for the following five). On the other hand, certain aspects of planning may be more detailed than others. For example, the firm planting forests as a basis for producing timber, pulp, and paper products may require detailed forestation plans for many years ahead, detailed re-equipment plans for its paper mills for a shorter but still long period, detailed paper product marketing plans for an even shorter period.

Long-term financial planning should ensure that an adequate amount of money is available to the firm up to the selected planning horizon. This ensures that, on the one hand, no project is in danger of being starved of financial resources before it reaches fruition, and that, on the other, no project is commenced without reasonable prospects for successful completion. This is the object of the exercise—successful completion. Therefore we need to plan sufficiently far ahead to accomplish this.

5.4   FORMAT OF THE FORECAST

In Chapter 2 we had introduced the two basic methods of measuring cash flow, the cash book method and the cash tank method. In our analysis of the principles of short-term cash forecasting in Chapter 3, the cash book method was recommended as this more nearly met the objectives of short-term cash forecasting and also provided a more useful framework for monitoring short-term cash flows and initiating management control action. When we come to the long-term cash forecast we have quite different objectives in view. These were spelled out earlier in this chapter but the significant point is that the long-term cash forecast is not concerned with predicting detailed cash receipts and cash payments. Rather it is concerned with revealing the financial consequences of management's strategic plans. For this reason, the cash tank method of analysis normally will be found to be more compatible with the needs of long-term cash forecasting because this method of analysis highlights decision areas rather than receipts and payments. The cash tank itself appeared in Figure 2.4 and the framework for analysis in Figure 2.5. This framework is reproduced again in Figure 5.1 but this time in the context of a suggested framework for preparing a long-term cash forecast.

However, if the framework is put together in the manner portrayed in Figure 5.1, it might usefully assist the preparation of a long-term cash forecast; but all it represents is a list of inflows and outflows of cash tabulated so as to reveal their net effect on the long-term requirements of financing. But long-term planning is concerned with the inter-relationship of different management plans and with management responsibility for such plans. Moreover, the impact

Line no.		1976	1977	1978	1979	1980
	INFLOWS OF CASH					
1	Operations before tax					
	New sources of capital:					
2	Long-term financing					
3	Additional supplier credit					
	Liquidation of surplus assets:					
4	Sale of fixed assets					
	Reduction of current assets:					
5	Decrease in inventories					
6	Reduction of customer credit					
7	TOTAL INFLOWS (I)					
	OUTFLOWS OF CASH					
8	Tax payment					
9	Dividend payment					
10	Interest payment					
11	Repayment of capital					
12	Reduction of supplier credit					
	Acquisition of assets:					
13	Purchase of fixed assets					
	Build-up of current assets:					
14	Increase in inventories					
15	Additional customer credit					
16	TOTAL OUTFLOWS (O)					
17	CURRENT SURPLUS (DEFICIT) (I - O)					
18	Cash and bank balances at end of previous year					
19	CASH AND BANK BALANCES AT END OF CURRENT YEAR					

Figure 5.1 Forecast of cash movements using the cash tank method

that operational and financial plans, respectively, have upon the future economic viability of the firm should be of more than passing interest. Surely, therefore, the way in which the long-term cash forecast is put together ought to reveal these inter-relationships and, if possible, it should also separate the impact of operational and financial strategies. All of this can quite easily be accomplished by drawing out a series of significant subtotals which reveal certain critical staging posts both in the requirement for and in the provision of long-term financing. The following staging posts could prove to be helpful:

Stage 1 *Potential cash flow from operations before tax,* i.e. the amount of cash that operating management expects to generate through production and selling activities, unadulterated by tax or financing decisions (over which they have no control) or by other asset and liability movements set in motion by these activities.

Stage 2 *Internally generated cash flow,* i.e. Stage 1 less the tax on corporate

130

profits which must be paid. This stage represents the amount of cash that current operations are able to generate for internal consumption.

Stage 3 *Operating cash profile,* i.e. Stage 2 less the necessary investment (or plus the disinvestment) in additional fixed assets, services, inventories, and customer credit that will be necessary to achieve the level of activity assumed at Stage 1. This stage indicates whether the operational activities of the firm are self-supporting, whether they require the input of additional finance, or whether they are providing a surplus.

Stage 4 *Total cash requirement (or surplus),* i.e. Stage 3 further adjusted for nonoperating financial obligations such as the payment of interest and dividends, significant payments under leasing contracts and necessary repayments of borrowing or preferred stock. It is not impossible for Stage 3 to be positive and Stage 4 to be negative. However, this could be an undesirable situation as it indicates that current operations are unable to support the chosen financial policy and further financing will become necessary simply to provide for financial obligations.

Stage 5a *Financing of Stage 4 requirements,* i.e. the detailed proposals for funding any requirement revealed at Stage 4, analyzed between
    1. *Changes in current position,* e.g. the reduction of cash balances, short-term investments, bank deposits, and other near-cash items.
    2. *Additional supplier credit,* if possible separating amounts automatically created by achievement of the level of activity assumed at Stage 1 from planned extensions of credit not associated with changes in the value of purchases.
    3. *New financing,* showing separately common stock or preferred stock, long-term borrowing and short-term borrowing. Entries here will help to determine future financial obligations.

Stage 5b *Utilization of Stage 4 surplus,* i.e. the proposals for dealing with any surplus revealed at Stage 4. Normally, this will be channelled into temporary investments as any long-term surplus would no doubt be used for retirement of outstanding borrowings.

The framework reproduced in Figure 5.2 incorporates the staging posts traced above and, as a format for the long-term cash forecast, is to be preferred to the less helpful list of inflows and outflows of cash that appeared in Figure 5.1.

Line no.		1976	1977	1978	1979	1980
1	Potential cash flow from operations					
2	*Less* Tax on corporate profits					
3	Internally generated cash flow					
	Less Increase/*Add* Decrease in:					
4	Land and buildings					
5	Plant and equipment					
6	Inventories					
7	Customer credit					
8	Operating cash profile					
	Less Financial obligations:					
9	Interest					
10	Capital repayment					
11	Lease payments					
12	Preference (preferred) dividends					
13	Equity (common) dividends					
14	TOTAL CASH REQUIREMENT					
	Planned financing:					
15	Reduction of cash and near-cash items					
16	Additional supplier credit					
17	New short-term borrowing					
18	New long-term borrowing					
19	New preference (preferred) capital					
20	New equity capital					
21	TOTAL PLANNED FINANCING (as line 14)					

Figure 5.2 Long-term forecast of cash requirements

5.5 SOURCE OF INPUT INFORMATION

We turn now to the process of putting numbers onto our suggested form. A long-term cash forecast reflects the collective financial consequences of all the individual long-term plans and therefore whatever workings are available for these plans will provide detailed input to the format reproduced in Figure 5.2. However the following specific comments refer to certain items on this form:

Line 1 *Potential cash flow from operations*—This is the projected profit from operations before deducting lease payments, interest, and tax, but also (as demonstrated in Chapter 1) is before charging depreciation.

Line 2 *Tax on corporate profits*—On this line appears the anticipated *payment* of corporate tax. This is not necessarily the blind application of standard corporate tax rates to Line 1 due to the possible incidence of significant tax reliefs and investment incentives. Nor does the payment necessarily refer to the profit arising for the year in which the payment is made; there may be a legally permissible delay in settlement. Indeed, in the case of United Kingdom firms, the

132

entries on this line will in all probability represent significantly the settlement of tax liability arising on profits of the preceding year.

Lines 4 and 5 *Land, buildings, plant, and equipment*—Here appear anticipated expenditures not only on direct production items but also on production service items, e.g. maintenance facilities, internal transport, and also on items to support administration, welfare, selling, distribution, research, and development activities. Clearly, all these projected payments are closely related to the capital expenditure budget.

Lines 6 and 7 *Inventories and customer credit*—A number of factors will form the basis for these projections. In the first place, a relationship will have been established in the past which will indicate the amounts which it is necessary to carry in order to service a given level of sales income. However this represents an average relationship and must not necessarily be projected indiscriminately into the future due to the following reasons:

1. Management may intend to change its policy either on the level of service it is prepared to provide from inventory or on the terms it is prepared to offer its customers. Such a change in policy will be reflected in a change in the relationship between movements in sales income and movements in inventories and customer credit balances.

2. Different products may require the different provision of inventory or credit support. For this reason, a significant shift in the product mix could again change the relationship between movements in sales income and movements in inventories and customer credit balances.

3. The impact of inflation must not be overlooked. The relationship established between sales income and amounts of inventory and credit to be carried may automatically take care of this matter provided that the incidence of inflation is uniform. However, it could be that inflation bears more heavily on some items than on others and this again could cause the established relationship to be distorted. Many firms in both the United Kingdom and U.S.A. found themselves in an unexpected liquidity crisis in the mid-1970s due to the rapid acceleration in rates of inflation which characterized the decade. Values locked up in inventories escalated without a corresponding escalation in volumes.

Lines 9 to 13 *Financial obligations*—The items in these lines will arise from the existing capital structure and from any changes to the capital structure planned in Lines 17 to 20. The term "obligation" is relative—clearly the equity (or common) dividend in Line 13 is a policy decision rather than a legally enforceable obligation. It is suggested that lease payments are more appropriately incorporated in this section rather than incorporated in those expenses deducted in arriving at line 1. Lease payments are more in the nature of an obligation arising from an "off the balance sheet" method of financing rather than an expense of operating the item which has been leased.

Line 15 *Reduction of cash and near cash*—This line represents the planned reduction of cash and bank balances and also the sale of investments held for conversion into cash. Management may prefer to retain certain balances as a tactical reserve in case of emergency rather than plan to utilize them all to the full. The problem of planning for financial emergencies will be taken further in a later chapter. Should Line 14 have revealed a temporary surplus, the investment of such surplus could conveniently be accommodated into Line 15 as a negative item.

Line 16 *Additional supplier credit*—Comments similar to those made at Lines 6 and 7 above are appropriate here when referring to the planned increase in customer credit. It is important to specify whether the additional supplier credit represents normal self-generation of additional finance created by a higher level of purchases or whether it represents a policy decision to seek an extension of current credit terms with some or all of the firm's suppliers.

Lines 17 to 20 *New external sources of finance (borrowings and share capital)*— These items represent the outcome of one of the essential elements of the firm's financial strategy. The basis for the financing decision which determines these items will be considered in a later chapter.

5.6 OPERATIONAL VERSUS FINANCIAL STRATEGIES

Earlier we observed that the main objectives of the long-term cash forecast are to ascertain the financial consequences of future operational plans and to assist in the selection of that long-term pattern of financing which must be developed in order to achieve the operational plans which have been chosen. In this context, it would seem that the long-term financial plan is determined by, or at least follows, the long-term operational plan. Indeed, this is most frequently the case and thus the art of financial management is to select that financial strategy or strategies which will most efficiently support the firm's operational strategy or strategies. However let us dwell for a moment on those occasions which might arise where the best financial strategy finds itself in conflict with the best operational strategy. If such occasions should arise, the firm must decide which strategy shall take priority—the operational or the financial. Should the more normal roles be reversed and the financial strategy find itself dictating to, or at least leading, the operational strategy, the long-term cash forecast will take on quite a different look.

Before taking our discussion further, perhaps it would be valuable to reflect upon an acceptable interpretation of the profit motive for a firm because, although we are concerned in this book with cash flow, we should not forget that a firm also needs to be profitable in the long term. But from whose point of view should profitability be regarded? In the capitalist society which is presently accepted in large parts of the Western world, and in which a relatively free stock market exists, the ultimate test of the adequacy of profitability is its acceptability to shareholders. Thus, it is argued that their point of view should prevail. The problem is that the shareholders' ultimate satisfaction comes from both current dividend and long-term enhancement in the market value of their shares. It is difficult to define what creates enhanced share values, but undoubtedly the following elements must be present:

1 The profit trend (retrospectively and prospectively) generated by the result of operational management's actions.

2 Other more financially based views of the firm. For example, share values would be affected by unannounced violent changes in established dividend policy, by reappraisal of the riskiness of the share in the light of the developing relationship between share capital and borrowings, or by evidence or rumor of a liquidity crisis. All these are the result of financial management's actions.

3 Other factors, mainly economic and political, which are beyond the control of management.

The reason for this diversion into the basis of share valuation is to underline the fact that a financial strategy can of itself affect share values (the shareholder's ultimate test of profitability) through element (2) above. Therefore, financial management is not only concerned with ensuring adequate funds to meet the needs of operational management, it is also concerned with the ultimate measure of profitability—enhanced share values. Herein most frequently lie the roots of conflict between operational and financial strategies.

Having undertaken our brief diversion, let us return to some examples where the long-term operational and financial strategies may come into conflict with each other, and where management must decide whether the financial strategy shall follow or dictate the operational:

1 A relatively straightforward example concerns the speed of operational growth. "Going for growth" of say 25 percent in one year may be both operationally acceptable and profitable. However, its impact on the need for additional funds arising from accelerated cash outflows on fixed assets and working capital could so distort the capital structure as to adversely affect share values. In these circumstances, it might be more desirable to go for the 25 percent growth target over a longer period of time and so smooth out the need for funds into a pattern more acceptable to the long-run capital structure of the firm. A firm must decide whether to select a growth pattern and seek funds to achieve it or whether to select a financial structure and permit growth only to the amount of funds thereby available.

2 Product mix is a critical determinant of total corporate cash flow and financing requirements. For this reason, an operational growth plan based upon one product mix may be financially viable yet the same volume of operational growth based upon a different product mix may be totally unacceptable to financial management for the same reasons as indicated in example (1). The problem is closely related to the product life cycle. In the early stages of a product's life, it is unlikely to generate cash in excess of its early investment requirements, yet towards the end of a successful life it displays the characteristics of a "cash cow" when it becomes a prolific generator of cash flow well in excess of its reinvestment requirements. In between these two extremes, a product may be moving rapidly towards becoming tomorrow's cash cow or unhappily it might stagnate and contribute little cash flow. Worse still, it may act as a net drain on corporate cash flow. In the ideal situation, the latter product will not exist and new product developments will be financed from cash cows. Thus, the whole operation becomes self-financing. However, if the mix gets out of balance, or operational plans indicate that the mix might get out of balance, the need to maintain a favorable financial position once more might dictate a desirable change to the orientation of operational plans.

3 What remains of internally generated cash flow, after having met financial obligations with the exception of dividends is, generally speaking, available either for operational investment (in either fixed assets, inventories, or customer credit) or for dividends; the lower the dividend, the more is available for operational investment. Yet the lower the dividend, the more disenchanted might shareholders become with this manifestation of corporate parsimony. Therefore, a firm may be faced with an unpalatable decision: shall it give priority to operational investment leaving the balance of internally generated cash flow, if any, for dividend and risk the consequences to its share values; or shall it determine how much it must pay in dividends to keep face with shareholders leaving the balance, if any, for operational investment?

4 The need to make the best use of the geographical disposition of internally generated cash flow and/or profits might dictate the nature of operational developments. Reference has already been made to the problem created when cash flow is generated in countries which restrict the free transferability of cash. A cash surplus might exist in country A while, at the same time, operational plans have to be shelved in country B due to a shortage of cash in that country. Alternatively, expansion may be contemplated in country A merely to take ad-

vantage of its favorable cash flow situation. Similar difficulties might arise due to the location of taxable profits. The British American Tobacco Company Limited is a case in point. In the early 1970s, almost the whole of BAT's profits arose outside the United Kingdom and yet the whole of its dividend was paid from inside the United Kingdom. A change in the method of computation of United Kingdom corporate tax forced upon BAT the need for rapid creation of United Kingdom profits if it were henceforth to minimize its worldwide tax liabilities. There is no doubt that the financially based tax considerations were a critically determining factor in the selection of appropriate operational strategies for this company at that time.

5   In an extreme case, financial considerations might indeed dictate the course of operational development. Three simple examples serve as illustrations:

  a. A small firm primarily concerned with repairing motor vehicles found itself in constant liquidity problems due to difficulties over credit control of collections from customers. Its decision to develop a taxicab operation in addition to its primary operation was dictated entirely by the desire to create a constant weekly source of *cash* income.

  b. A medium sized manufacturer of specialized motor delivery vehicles traditionally saw its role as the provision of a complete manufacturing service. Financial considerations, primarily related to the financing of inventories, forced it to change its strategy from complete manufacture to an assembler of major sub-contracted sub-assemblies.

  c. A large manufacturer of confectionery products made a successful take-over bid for another manufacturer and thereby found itself also the owner of a wholesale warehousing operation. Because wholesale warehousing was not part of its agreed operational strategy ("What business are we in?"). This activity became a candidate for divestment. But these things take time to organize and, in the meantime, the manufacturer began to reap the benefits of the peculiarly advantageous cash flow situation of one who buys on credit and sells for cash. So its operational strategy has now been broadened to embrace wholesale warehousing.

These are a few, and there will be other, specific examples of potential conflict or difference in orientation between ongoing operational and financial strategies—where management must assess its priorities on an ad hoc basis. However, let us take as our final example the situation where a firm is quite clearly financially rather than operationally oriented. To many managements this is an unacceptable strategy, yet many firms have achieved spectacular growth trends from an orientation towards growth in shareholder value and have forced operational strategies very clearly into second place. Many of the early conglomorates represent classic examples of purely financially oriented companies. Some have failed disastrously but many operationally oriented companies have also failed equally disastrously, so we must not be too hard on the financial whiz kids or wheeler-dealers. A firm must realize and accept that part of its long-term planning responsibility is to determine an acceptable relationship between operational and financial strategies—and to develop its long-term cash forecast accordingly.

5.7 REPORTING CASH MOVEMENTS

We have seen how both operational and financial management can make their impact upon cash flow, and earlier in this chapter we reviewed a format for preparing a long-term forecast which is designed to highlight the relative contributions of these different management functions, and hence to reveal the quality of management performance. If a firm finds itself in financial difficulties, is this due to operational management action (and if so, is it lack of potential cash flow from trading or excessive capital requirement) or to financial management action, e.g. the stubborn adherence to an overly generous dividend policy?

When a company reports cash movements to interested parties, would it not be more helpful to report in such a way that the reader can also assess these relative contributions by management? At the end of Chapter 2, we briefly reviewed the state of the art in reporting cash movements to interested parties outside the firm and reproduced an example of United States and United Kingdom reporting. At that time, we promised to return to the subject and suggest an alternative structure for presenting the report. It should now be apparent that, for the reasons just given, the quality of the published statement of source and application of funds would be considerably improved if the five-stage format outlined in this chapter as a basis for long-term forecasting were also to be used as a basis for reporting historical movements in cash flow in the published accounts of limited companies. Surely, shareholders deserve to know not only the state of liquidity of their company and how it got into that state, but also who was responsible for getting there. Two further examples of reporting are shown in Figures 5.3 and 5.4. Both examples mark an interesting move in the direction suggested above.

UNITED TECHNOLOGIES CORPORATION AND SUBSIDIARIES

CONSOLIDATED STATEMENT OF CHANGES IN FINANCIAL POSITION

For the Two Years Ended December 31, 1977

	1977	1976
	(Thousands of Dollars)	
Sources of Working Capital:		
Operations:		
Net income	$195,972	$ 157,403
Items not requiring working capital:		
Depreciation	99,837	91,409
Minority interests in subsidiaries' earnings	13,202	13,736
Retirement of fixed assets	7,179	18,114
Change in long-term receivables, and other	(4,386)	26,573
Total from operations	$311,804	$ 307,235
Proceeds, and tax benefit, under employee incentive stock plans	14,943	15,953
Preferred Stock issued on merger with Otis	—	121,616
Stock issued on conversion of debentures	82,061	50,591
Miscellaneous	3,942	—
	$412,750	$ 495,395
Uses of Working Capital:		
Investment in and advances to unconsolidated finance subsidiary	$ 344	$ 1,983
Additions to fixed assets	145,405	131,174
Acquisition of minority interest in Otis	—	114,289
Long-term debt maturing	13,635	16,192
Long-term debt repaid prior to maturity	11,297	208,583
Cash dividends on Common and Preferred Stock	80,777	58,590
Conversion of debentures	82,061	50,591
Miscellaneous	—	4,948
	$333,519	$ 586,350
Increase (decrease) in working capital	$ 79,231	$ (90,955)
Changes in Working Capital:		
Increase (decrease) in current assets:		
Cash and short-term cash investments	$236,654	$ 139,759
Accounts receivable	45,415	(115,361)
Future income tax benefits	5,002	(521)
Inventories and contracts in progress, net	9,882	(134,122)
Prepaid expenses	4,687	(2,641)
	$301,640	$(112,886)
Increase (decrease) in current liabilities:		
Short-term borrowings	$(13,259)	$ (34,827)
Accounts payable	24,350	(23,578)
Accrued liabilities	94,912	43,440
Long-term debt—currently due	(2,557)	2,731
Income taxes	49,982	21,568
Advances on sales contracts	68,981	(31,265)
	$222,409	$ (21,931)
Increase (decrease) in working capital	$ 79,231	$ (90,955)

Figure 5.3 United Technologies Corporation and Subsidiaries—consolidated statement of changes in financial position ended December 31 (in thousands of dollars)

UNITED STATES STEEL CORPORATION
STATEMENT OF CHANGES IN FINANCIAL POSITION

	(In millions)	
	1977	1976
Additions to working capital		
Income	$ 137.9	$ 410.3
Add—Wear and exhaustion of facilities	372.0	308.6
Deferred taxes on income	47.1	116.9
Funds from operations	557.0	835.8
Issuance of convertible subordinated debentures	—	400.0
Increases in other long-term debt due after one year	577.5	142.8
Proceeds from sales of common stock	72.7	41.3
Proceeds from sales and salvage of plant and equipment	71.2	17.1
Issuance of preferred stock of consolidated subsidiary	250.0	—
Total additions	1,528.4	1,437.0
Deductions from working capital		
Expended for plant and equipment	864.7	957.3
Increases in investments and long-term receivables	10.1	160.4
Dividends on common stock	182.4	172.8
Decreases in long-term debt due after one·year	237.2	125.4
Increases in costs applicable to future periods	47.3	70.2
Miscellaneous deductions	12.7	9.8
Total deductions	1,354.4	1,495.9
Increase (decrease) in working capital	$ 174.0	$ (58.9)

ANALYSIS OF INCREASE (DECREASE) IN WORKING CAPITAL

	1977	1976
Working capital at beginning of year	$1,153.8	$1,212.7
Cash and marketable securities	138.3	(121.2)
Receivables, less doubtful accounts	243.1	36.4
Inventories	(132.3)	216.4
Notes payable	(23.4)	(79.2)
Accounts payable	(28.3)	(51.6)
Payroll and benefits payable	(36.7)	(110.6)
Accrued taxes	44.6	71.3
Long-term debt due within one year	(31.3)	(20.4)
Increase (decrease) in working capital	174.0	(58.9)
Working capital at end of year	$1,327.8	$1,153.8

Figure 5.4 United States Steel Corporation—statement of changes in financial position and analysis of increase (decrease) in working capital (in millions)

140

Wenman Plastics:
Part 5

Before reading this part of the case study, readers are first invited to review the earlier parts and especially their views in response to Question 7 (Part 4).

Claude Wenman was anxious to produce an early estimate of possible cash requirements by Wenman Plastics so that he could assure his father and himself that his scheme for the development of the company was economically viable in the long term. Moreover, if it became necessary to look outside the firm for additional longer-term financing it would be necessary to give some clear indication of possible repayment dates. In order to develop his first long-term cash forecast, he felt that the following sequence represented a reasonably practical approach to the problem:

1 Determine the starting point.

2 Determine the ultimate objective.

3   Consider an appropriate time scale.

4   Develop the long-term cash forecast.

The Starting Point

A first cash forecast had been produced for the year ending March 31, 1974 (see Exhibits 5 and 6, Part 3). This would form the basis of discussion with his father and until they had decided what, if any, policy changes were desirable and acceptable he felt that this was a useful starting point. This forecast represented the first year of operation at an annual sales level of $6 million and indicated appropriate requirements not only for operating expenses but also for fixed assets and working capital.

The Ultimate Objective

Claude had spent considerable effort in researching the market for his new product range. It seemed to him that there was tremendous potential to develop the market to several times his initial projection of sales for 1974. He realized that competition must develop, despite his patent protection, but, nevertheless believed that an annual sales level target of at least $10–12 million was achievable by Wenman Plastics and would represent a not too ambitious share of the total market potential. However on reviewing the present production facilities it became clear that limitations of both space and production capacity with three shifts working would not permit expansion of sales beyond $10 million without a further capital expenditure program of similar magnitude to that currently planned for 1973. For these reasons, and also because he felt that his father might consider $10 million of sales to be 'big enough,' he selected this level of sales as his ultimate objective.

Claude realized that economies of scale should really pay off at the $10 million level and, therefore, in order to link the starting point with the ultimate objective, he projected a profit statement at that level based upon his original estimates for 1974 developed as necessary to reveal what he believed to be achievable at the higher level of sales. The result of his projections is reproduced as Exhibit 7. He was aware that the low percentage profit estimated for the year to March 31, 1974 was caused largely by the high proportion of overheads necessary to get the project off the ground and he was pleased to note the percentage profit that should be achievable at the higher level of sales.

Estimate 1974 as Exhibit 2			Projection to $10 million	
$'000s	%		$'000s	%
5,250	100	Sales	10,000	100.0
		Less Direct cost of sales:		
1,733	33	Materials	3,400	34.0
1,312	25	Labor	2,600	26.0
2,205	42	Gross margin	4,000	40.0
480	9	Salaries and related expenses	630	6.3
400	8	Rent, rates, electricity and telephone	420	4.2
		Other running expenses:		
250	5	Production	280	2.8
120	2	Administration	180	1.8
80	1.5	Advertising	120	1.2
80	1.5	Selling and distribution	140	1.4
795	15	Potential cash flow from operations	2,230	22.3
300	6	Deduct depreciation charge	430	4.3
$495	9%	Profit before interest and tax	$1,800	18%

Exhibit 7 Wenman Plastics—estimated profit statement at sales of $10 million

The Time-Scale

Moving the sales from $6 million to $10 million could not be accomplished overnight and although Claude was anxious to have the business generate a positive cash flow as early as possible, he believed that five years would be a realistic time-scale over which to reach his ultimate objective. On this basis, it seemed reasonable to aim for the following annual level of sales in each year ended March 31 up to his planning horizon:

1974 $6,000,000—initial estimate

1975 $6,500,000—moderate increase to allow for establishment of market

1976 $7,500,000—more rapid rate of increase as the market takes off

1977 $8,500,000—more rapid rate of increase as the market takes off

1978 $9,000,000—moderate increase allowing for development of new market areas and ultimate shift working in production

1979 $10,000,000—the ultimate objective achieved in 5 years.

Developing the Long-Term Forecast

Armed with the information developed above and in Exhibit 7 and assuming requirements for fixed assets and working capital proportional to what he had projected for his initial estimate to March 31, 1974, Claude was now able to

143

develop a forecast of cash requirements through to 1979. He was concerned to reveal not only the net cash surplus or deficit each year but also the staging posts by which this had arisen, e.g. how much from operations, how much from financial obligations, and so on. The result of this work is reproduced as Exhibit 8.

Claude realized that Exhibit 8 represented the first rough attempt at a long-term cash forecast but it was getting late and it would suffice as an addition to the material for discussion with his father the following day. In particular, he thought of the fact that financial obligations in the first two years were in excess of the operating cash profile and again considered his father's insistence on maintaining the dividend payout. He was happy to see that by 1979 the business would have generated not only sufficient cash to reimburse the initial deficit but would also permit Wenman Plastics to begin repayment of the secured loan. Moreover, he saw the columns on his forecast not so much representing years as the cash flow outcome of different levels of sales income. For this reason, the cumulative cash deficit would presumably be eliminated sooner if it were possible to achieve the $10 million level of sales any earlier than 1979. In any event, there seemed to be no need to look for anything but medium-term financing. Karl would no doubt be relieved that it should not yet be necessary to offer additional share capital for sale after all.

Exhibit 8   Wenman Plastics—long-term cash forecast 1975–1979

1974 $'000s		1975 $'000s	1976 $'000s	1977 $'000s	1978 $'000s	1979 $'000s
$5,250	Sales	$6,500	$7,500	$8,500	$9,000	$10,000
795	Potential cash flow from operations	1,100	1,390	1,665	1,770	2,230
(15%)	(% sales)	(17%)	(19%)	(20%)	(20%)	(22%)
150	Payment of tax (previous year's liability)	200	300	400	550	600
645	Internally generated cash flow	900	1,090	1,265	1,220	1,630
1,000	Purchase of plant, equipment and vehicles	420	450	490	520	530
555	Increase in inventories	245	200	200	100	200
432	Additional customer credit	20	150	200	50	200
(1,342)	Operating cash profile	215	290	375	550	700
	Payment of interest:					
72	On secured loan	72	72	72	72	72
–	On deficit financing (est.)	120	120	100	50	20
100	Payment of dividend	100	100	110	120	135
(1,514)	Total cash (requirement)/ surplus	(77)	(2)	93	308	473
270	Additional supplier credit	47	50	75	25	75
110	Sale of surplus assets	–	–	–	–	–
450	Secured loan	–	–	–	–	–
$ (684)	Total (deficit)/surplus	$ (30)	$48	$168	$333	$548
$ (684)	Cumulative (deficit)/surplus	$(714)	$(666)	$(498)	$(165)	$383

Question 8

How much faith do you place in Claude's long-term cash forecast? Could there possibly be any understatement or overstatement of the forecast need for additional financing? Are there any margins of safety here?

Question 9

What policy decisions would you now recommend to Karl and Claude?

Question 10

What financing arrangements would you recommend Wenman Plastics to seek?

6

Management of Long-Term Financing

If the long-term cash forecast reveals
that a need for additional funds will arise
in the future, the problem presents itself
of how best to fill this need. A wide choice of sources
of financing is in fact available
but a detailed itemization and description
of each source is beyond the scope of this book.
Moreover, any attempt at itemization
would quickly become dated because
specific new sources appear and old ones disappear
with remarkable frequency as the economic environment
and the ingenuity of the financial community wax and wane
in different parts of the world.
However, there are certain basic general principles
which management should follow in order to manage
its long-term need for financing to the best advantage of the firm.
These general principles will be considered in this chapter.

6.1 SPECTRUM OF SOURCES OF FINANCING

The cash forecast will reveal if, when, for how long, and in what amounts additional financing might be required in the future. It is the responsibility of financial management to obtain that financing on the most economical terms and in such a way as not to put in jeopardy the continued economic viability of the firm. In fact, there is a wide selection of sources of financing almost constantly available, almost in any amount and to meet almost any need . . . but at a price. Thus, the problem frequently facing financial management is not whether funds can be raised but where they shall be raised.

Although there is a wide selection of individual sources of financing available, many are of a similar type and, because it is the type of source rather than the specific method of financing which is of the greater concern to the financing decision, let us concentrate our attention in this chapter on the spectrum of types of financing that are available. There are many different methods of classifying this spectrum. In fact, the three main inlet pipes to our cash tank (introduced in Chapter 2 and demonstrated in Section 2.3) represent one method of classification, *viz:*

1 Potential cash flow from operations.

2 New financing.

3 Liquidation of surplus assets.

However, this method of classification is designed as a basis for analyzing and controlling cash flows. In this chapter, because we are concerned with the financing decision, let us reconsider the spectrum and reclassify it in the following outline:

1 Internal sources:
    a. potential cash flow from trading operations,
    b. liquidation of surplus assets.

2 Normal external domestic sources:
    a. resulting in an entry on the balance sheet:
      i.   "free" capital,
      ii. capital serviced by interest, i.e. borrowed capital,
      iii. capital serviced by dividends, i.e. share capital;
    b. "off the balance sheet" financing, e.g. leasing.

3 Special domestic sources, e.g. the government, or other trading organizations.

4 External foreign sources—all of the domestic sources within bands (2) and (3) will be repeated here.

Let us look a little more deeply into each of these bands of the spectrum and consider the decision rules that financial management might adopt in making its selection from the spectrum of sources open to it.

6.2 INTERNAL SOURCES OF FINANCING

This source should not be overlooked: if additional financing is required, there is often an irresistible desire to look outside the firm immediately. However, internal sources should always be considered first because they should normally be cheaper than external sources. Moreover, financing from within provides the opportunity to redeploy existing funds so as to achieve a more efficient utilization of capital.

Potential cash flow from operations is, of course, the continuing internal source of funds but this might not flow in quickly enough to satisfy the demands being placed upon it. Alternatively, it may arise in, and be tied down in, a foreign country which restricts the repatriation of capital and hence be unavailable for domestic needs. Despite the existence of cash flow from operations, therefore, a firm might still have to look to an external source as a bridging operation.

Liquidation of surplus assets represents a once-off (or one-time) internal source of funds which becomes available from time to time. The obvious example is the outright sale of buildings, plant, equipment, inventories, or other investments, the ongoing performance of which no longer justifies the continued employment of the liquidation value of finance locked up in them. Wise management should continuously be on the look out for such possibilities within the firm even to the extent of maintaining an "assassination list" or "euthanasia list" of items of doubtful value which might be called upon by liquidation in case of need. However, there is a further aspect to the liquidation of assets which must not be overlooked, namely the running down or reduction in the level of working capital items required for operational purposes—mainly inventories, cash balances, and receivables or debts. Reductions here represent either a genuine source of financing through the creation of an inflow of cash or an effective source of financing through the prevention of a further outflow of cash.

6.3 SELECTION OF AN EXTERNAL SOURCE OF FINANCING

Within the external bands of the spectrum the greatest breadth of selection occurs: sources of varying type, length, conditions, and cost present themselves; many different bodies and financial institutions offer their services. However, the selection is not always free and open. At certain times, or under certain circumstances, an individual source may or may not be open to a prospective seeker of financing. Many factors will come to bear on the availability, or suitability, of each particular source including the following:

1 Why the financing is required.

2 Status of the firm seeking the financing.

3 Initial cost of obtaining financing.

'. . .there is a wide selection of
sources of finance almost constantly available, almost in any amount,
and to meet almost any need. . .'

4 Future financial obligations thereby created.

5 Other obligations and restrictions also created.

6 Economic and market environment.

Let us consider in turn how each of these factors might affect the selection of an external source of financing.

6.3.1 Why the Financing Is Required

It is clearly as illogical to raise a twenty year secured loan to provide for a temporary extension of customer credit as it is to seek short-term bank facilities to finance the building of a new factory. As far as possible, an external source of finance must be compatible with the use to which it will be put. This means that for certain needs, certain areas of the spectrum of sources of financing will be closed. The link between use and source frequently is created by the duration of the need, as in the two simple examples just given, but this is not always the case. Certain uses, e.g. the construction of a ship or the purchase of timberland, create unique opportunities or specific assets which in turn create security or other justification for a particular source of financing which would not other-wise be available. Certain uses would be attractive to specialized financial institu-tions which have been created to meet the needs of such uses, e.g. the United Kingdom body EDITH (The Estate Duties Investment Trust Limited), which

150

specializes in assisting those small firms that need to raise funds to meet the pressing needs of death duties. Certain uses at certain times would qualify for special government assistance, e.g. the practice of many governments to assist investment in certain specified underdeveloped areas. A prospective provider of financing will certainly look differently upon uses which create additional administrative facilities, to uses which create additional revenue earning capacity, to uses which simply represent maintenance of existing production facilities, or to uses which represent the repayment of existing borrowings. Thus, in many ways, the reason why the financing is required might largely determine its source.

6.3.2   Status of the Firm Seeking Financing

If the firm seeking financing does not represent an attractive proposition to the prospective provider of funds, then it will be difficult to conclude a financing arrangement in certain areas of the spectrum of sources. Many factors come to bear here, for example:

1   What is the legal status of the firm seeking financing? Is it a sole trade or proprietorship (in which case it will no doubt suffer the greatest restriction of choice)? Is it a partnership? Is it a limited liability company or corporation (in which case it has potentially the widest choice depending on whether it is a private or a publicly quoted company and whether its shares are actively traded in a recognized stock exchange)?

2   What is the financial status of the firm seeking financing? Is the firm profitable (historically, currently, or prospectively)? Is it financially sound or unsound? Is it already heavily dependent on debt financing or is there ample room for more?

3   What is the public or market image of the firm seeking financing? Is it large or small? Is it unknown, well-known, or indeed infamous? Is it an infant, a growth firm, or a sleeping giant? Does it have a good or bad credit rating?

4   What is the industrial status of the firm seeking financing? Is it in a "popular" or "unpopular" industry, e.g. tobacco before and after the lung cancer investigation? What traditional patterns of financing apply? Is it an expanding or contracting industry?

These and other "personal attributes" may permit one firm ready access to a particular source of financing that would be denied to another firm or may permit access at one point in time but not at another. Clearly, it is in a firm's interest to continuously cultivate the status or image that will enhance its acceptability to the widest range of potential providers of funds. The field of financial public relations is one which is growing and which can make an interesting and valuable contribution to effective management of long-term financing.

6.3.3 Initial Cost of Obtaining Financing

If any initial cost must be incurred in order to gain access to a particular source of finance, a larger amount than is required must be sought so that the required amount remains after payment of such cost. Some sources have a very high initial cost, e.g. the cost of raising money from shareholders. Others have a moderate initial cost, e.g. the commitment fee chargeable by some banks for providing overdraft or other credit facilities. Still others have no initial cost at all, e.g. the delay in payment of creditors, or payables. The higher the initial cost, the larger must be the sum raised if the exercise is to be worthwhile. It therefore follows that those areas in the spectrum of financing sources with the highest initial cost would only be used for the larger requirements for financing. For example, in order to raise money from shareholders through a public offer for sale or prospectus issue, a high initial cost would be incurred to cover the printing of documents, advertising, mailing, accountants', lawyers', brokers', registrars', and bankers' fees, underwriting commission, government fees, or duties. The final total depends to a great extent on the level of advertising undertaken and the resultant response solicited from the public. The initial costs of a rights issue to existing shareholders would be lower as such an issue would not incur the heavy advertising and printing costs of a public offer for sale. The various professional fees are also likely to be lower. It is difficult to give an example of a typical figure for costs as no two funding operations are alike. Each has its own individual problems and requirements which, depending on their complexity, can significantly affect the level of the initial costs incurred.

6.3.4 Future Financial Obligations

Once a source of finance has been negotiated, a contractual or moral obligation exists for future cash outflows. Such an obligation could represent interest, dividends, capital repayment, or the servicing of a hire purchase, installment purchase, or lease agreement. Before taking on any obligation, management should at least ensure that the obligation can be met without putting the very existence of the firm in jeopardy. This, of course, implies the preparation of cash forecasts and related sensitivity analyses. Some sources of financing may represent greater risk than others. The following points in particular need to be considered when assessing the future financial obligations:

1 *The true net-of-tax per annum rate of service charge must be established.* Net of tax must be the criterion because some service charges, e.g. payments of interest, are wholly tax deductible but some are not, e.g. dividend payments. To a tax paying company for instance a 12 percent interest may be cheaper than a 10 percent dividend. Per annum must be the criterion because not all rates are quoted per annum. Borrowing from the bank at 12 percent is cheaper than offering a 2½ percent discount for prompt payment of otherwise 'net 30 days' debtors or accounts receivable because 12 percent implies 12 percent per annum but 2½ percent in this case is per month or 30 percent per annum. The service charge is not always clearly stated and may need careful extraction from a complex package as may be the case with hire purchase, installment purchase, or lease agreements. It is necessary to establish the true per annum service charge as a basis of comparison, but it does not follow that the source of financing with the lower service charge would be selected automatically as the following further points reveal. (For a slightly lower service charge the borrower may be buying considerably more risk or greater inflexibility).

2 *The degree of maneuverability in the service charge must be considered.* The rate may be fixed or it may decline or increase over the period of financing or it may or may not fluctuate with some external influence such as the base bank lending rate. The borrower may have the ability to postpone the service charge (as with a preferred dividend) but if not (as with debenture interest) the provider of financing may exercise certain sanctions which could cause considerable problems to the borrower.

3 *If the financing has to be repaid, the terms of repayment must also be considered.* Repayment may be at the discretion of the borrower and hence create a degree of freedom, or at the discretion of the lender and hence create uncertainty. Repayment may be stipulated in a pattern of periodic repayments or in a lump sum at a predetermined future date. The lump sum may or may not incorporate a premium element representing in effect a deferred and capitalized additional service charge. As an alternative to repayment some right may be offered to convert into another form of finance, e.g. a convertible debenture which is convertible at the option of the holder into equity shares. As with the service charge, it is necessary to consider the sanctions which the lender can impose should contractual repayment not be possible at the time or in the manner specified.

6.3.5 Other Obligations and Restrictions

Any source of financing represents a package, only part of which is the financial obligation thereby created. What else does the firm seeking financing get (or suffer) for its money? Perhaps the most critical nonfinancial part of the package is the loss or restriction of some freedom of action either immediately or potentially. Issue of, or conversion into, additional equity shares creates votes unless the shares are nonvoting of course. In a rights issue the balance of power will not be disturbed unless a significant proportion of the rights is sold to third parties, but in an issue to new shareholders a shift in control of the company could be created. Short of shareholders voting rights, other restrictions might be imposed. An institutional lender may demand a seat on the board as a condition to providing financing. Security pledged for a loan may deny to the borrower free and unrestricted use of some or all of his assets. As a condition for providing financing, the provider may demand creation of a legally binding document which among other things is designed to limit the volume and type of subsequent financing. Such a restriction will clearly alter the status of the firm (as described above) at the next round of financing. A supplier may be willing to provide financing but only in exchange for guarantees on the types of future financings. Thus, a source of financing that is apparently inexpensive on the face of it, may turn out to be highly expensive or undesirable in terms of the other obligations rolled into the package.

6.3.6 Economic and Market Environment

No situation is ever static. Indeed, funds must be raised within an environment that is constantly changing due to pressure and counter pressure from local, national, and international economic, political, and social forces. Areas of the spectrum of sources, of financing, might open and close under these shifting pressures, in particular:

1 Timing becomes a critical element when raising funds, particularly when interest rates tend to fluctuate. Some years ago a well-known multinational company was severely criticized for raising a long-term loan on the United Kingdom stock exchange at the then astronomically high interest rate of 10¾ percent. The subsequent escalation of interest rates coupled with the impact of accelerating inflation on the value of repayment at maturity proved the wisdom of that decision.

2 An issue of new shares needs to be carried out when the share value is high in order to minimize the number of shares to be issued. Therefore, share issues tend to be avoided when the stock market is depressed. Mistiming an issue of shares could prove expensive to shareholders in terms of dilution both of earnings and market value per share.

3 Fashion is a fickle phenomenon which changes over time and certain areas of the spectrum of sources of financing enjoy transient fashion; different sources

gain and lose popularity and hence open and close to the seeker of financing as time passes by. One particular method of raising funds from the public in the United Kingdom is by tender, as distinct from a fixed-price issue. This method was traditionally employed by United Kingdom water companies but in the 1960s blossomed into general use only to fade into obscurity again in a relatively short period of time. The coincidence of high rates of interest and inflation tends to increase the popularity of convertible forms of finance while that condition lasts.

So much for the general factors underlying the selection of an appropriate source of external financing. It is clear that this financing decision represents a complex mixture of many variables, both quantifiable and nonquantifiable. The outcome of this decision is to add a further parcel of funds to the existing mix of sources comprising the corporate pool of capital. The essential core of the financing decision, therefore, is to determine an appropriate mix for this pool—a mix that will be reflected in the firm's capital structure as revealed in the balance sheet. Therefore, let us now turn our attention to the specific elements in this mix, i.e. "free" capital, capital serviced by interest payments, capital serviced by dividend payments, and "off the balance sheet" financing.

6.4 USE OF "FREE" CAPITAL

"Free" capital is created mainly by delaying payment to creditors for materials supplied or services rendered. Certain other items, notably dividends and taxes, are legally subject to considerable delay in payment which provides a further useful source of temporary funds. Various aspects associated with the extraction of "free" capital from suppliers have been mentioned in an earlier chapter, but are worthy of repetition here. The capital is "free" in that it is not specifically serviced by either interest or dividend. However, very little is really free in this world! Presumably, the supplier has taken account of his normal credit terms in arriving at his selling price and, therefore, "free" capital is in effect serviced in the price which the supplier charges. Moreover, if credit is extended unreasonably beyond the normal credit terms there is real risk that the supplier will withhold supplies or take other sanctions against the customer when it is seen that the capital becomes quite expensive.

However, particularly because the supplier is effectively charging for this capital in his selling price, it seems sensible to take the maximum credit legally permissible. There would appear to be no particular merit in settling a supplier's account any earlier than is absolutely necessary, thereby replacing this "free" source of financing with another, such as bank borrowing, on which interest must be paid. On the other hand, if the supplier is prepared to offer a discount for prompt payment this must always be considered because the discount clearly puts a price tag upon this "free" element of capital and in effect converts it into serviced capital. If the supplier offers cash discount for prompt payment of such an amount representing an equivalent per annum rate which is higher than that charged on the cheapest available alternative remunerated source of financing, it will clearly be sensible to settle promptly and replace this "free" financing with the cheapest available alternative. For example, assume we normally pay a supplier in 60 days but he offers a 2½ percent discount for prompt cash. Bank borrowing is readily available at 12 percent. The offer by the supplier is equivalent to 2½ percent × (365/60) or 15 percent. Therefore, in this case it is worth increasing bank borrowing to take benefit of the cash discount. Had the supplier offered less than 2 percent it would not have been worth taking unless we normally pay in less than 60 days.

6.5 USE OF BORROWED CAPITAL

Borrowed capital or debt financing is that part of the capital structure which is serviced by paying interest. It presents to the seeker of financing perhaps the widest choice of individual sources while, at the same time, it presents to the financial manager a valuable opportunity for enhancement of the equity shareholder's value. Therefore, the decision to use debt financing is both critical to the firm and central to the whole art of financial management.

As has been stated already, there is a wide choice of individual sources of debt financing available to the firm. Bank credit facilities are the more common, on either a short- or medium-term basis. Loans are available from many private, corporate, and institutional sources while ultimately there is the debenture, or bond, put together by public subscription. Borrowing may be unsecured, secured by a fixed charge or lien on specific assets, or secured by a floating charge or claim on the firm's assets generally. There are many different possible ways of repayment or refunding. Some loans may be in the form of convertibles, i.e. the holder has the option to convert into equity shares on certain specified terms at a specified future date or dates. However, irrespective of the method or instrument of debt financing selected, all borrowing normally has the common feature of being serviced by a fixed rate of interest which represents a prior charge on profits ahead of any dividend.

It is, in fact, the fixed interest feature that creates potential for enhancement of equity share values. If the amount borrowed can be employed within the firm at a rate of return in excess of the cost of interest, then any such surplus adds to the parcel of earnings available to the equity shareholder without any corresponding addition to the equity capital base. An oversimplified example, ignoring taxation, will demonstrate the point: each of three companies has an operating profit, or "Earnings Before Interest and Tax" (EBIT), of $200. The equity shareholder in each case is entitled to what remains of the profit or earnings after deducting interest on the debt capital, i.e. subject to taxation, and is entitled to the "Earnings Before Tax" (EBT). Each company has a total capital of $1000 and so the operating profit represents a 20 percent return on total capital in each case. However, each company has a different proportion of debt within its capital structure: Company A, no debt; Company B, 20 percent; Company C, 50 percent. Figure 6.1 shows that although each company is earning the same 20 percent return on total capital, the equity shareholder is earning different returns on his capital (20 percent in Company A, 22½ percent in Company B, and 30 percent in Company C). This manifestation of the enhancement of equity share values is known as capital gearing, or leverage, and is further demonstrated in chart form for the same three companies in Figure 6.2. Notice that in A, any EBIT moves straight through to the benefit of equity; note, however, that in B and C the excess of EBIT over the cost of debt is transferred to equity as indicated by the shaded areas of the two charts. This transfer gears up the return to equity to 22½ percent in B but to 30 percent in C because the greater proportion of debt in this capital structure has transferred a greater area of excess earnings. Clearly, it follows that the greater the proportion of debt in the capital structure, i.e. the higher the gearing, the greater will be the return to equity for any given level of EBIT. It must also follow that the higher the level of EBIT for any given capital structure the greater will be the leverage and this is demonstrated in the graph in Figure 6.3 which again uses the same company's data. This graph relates EBIT to EBT for a considerable range of earnings; the

	Company A $	Company B $	Company C $
Equity capital ($1 shares)	1000	800	500
Debt capital	–	200	500
Total capital	$1000	$1000	$1000
EBIT (earnings before interest and tax)	200	200	200
Interest on debt, 10%	–	20	50
EBT (earnings before tax)	$200	$180	$150
EBIT % total capital	20%	20%	20%
EBT % equity capital*	20%	22.5%	30%
EPS (earnings per share) ignoring tax*	20	22.5	30

*Subject to taxation, equity shareholders are entitled to the earnings which remain after deducting interest.

Figure 6.1 Demonstration of the impact of capital gearing, or leverage, on the percentage return on equity capital

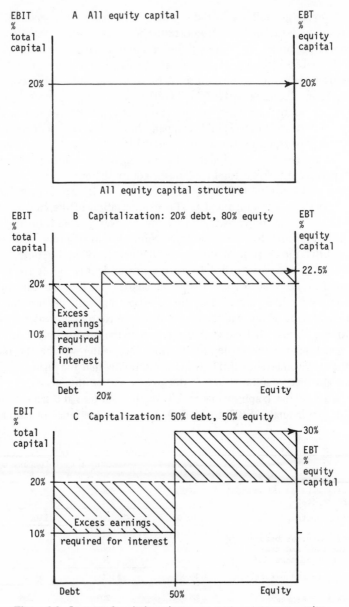

Figure 6.2 Impact of capital gearing on percentage return to equity

slope of the lines on the graph reflects the degree of gearing—the steeper the slope, the higher the gearing. Note that when EBIT is 20 percent of total capital the return to equity is 20 percent for A, 22½ percent for B, and 30 percent for C as already demonstrated in our example and in the charts in Figure 6.2. However, when EBIT moves to 40 percent of total capital the return to equity moves to 40, 47½ and 70 percent in Companies A, B, and C, respectively.

158

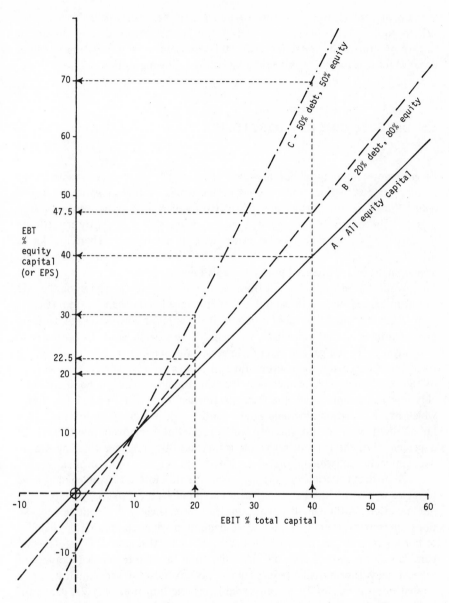

Figure 6.3 Impact of variation in earnings on percentage return to equity (or EPS)

But what goes up might come down! Figure 6.3 also demonstrates the downside risk of capital gearing or leverage. Note that a break-even point exists at 10 percent (the point where the return to equity and the return on total capital is the same in each case), but to the left of the break-even point the use of gearing rapidly accelerates the declining return to equity both down to zero and into the negative quadrants of the graph: a 5 percent EBIT to total capital creates a 5 percent return to equity in A but a zero return in C. It is this increased risk to equity which begins to highlight the critical nature of the decision to finance by borrowed capital. Moreover, this risk is not only reflected in potential negative returns to equity as we shall see in the following section.

6.6   DEVELOPMENT OF A DEBT POLICY

Given the upside potential but downside risk to equity shareholders, as described in the previous section, what should be the firm's attitude towards the use of debt? Are there any further benefits or risks which need to be weighed in the balance? Indeed there are, and it is necessary for a firm to clarify its attitude towards the benefits and risks associated with its use of debt. Therefore, let us briefly review some of the main elements that the firm ought to consider in the development of a formalized policy towards the use of debt.

While the principal benefit from the use of debt is its impact upon the rate of return earned on equity capital, a further, considerable, benefit from straight debt is the eroding influence of inflation. If the amount borrowed carries a fixed rate of interest, inflation will be working to the advantage of the borrower in two ways. First, the general level of interest rates might rise and, therefore, the fixed rate being paid could no doubt appear relatively inexpensive as years go by. Second, when repayment takes place the amount repaid will be of considerably lower real monetary value than it was when borrowed. In Brazil (a country which has suffered considerable rates of inflation), it is common to issue 'index linked' debt whereby the interest rate is pegged at a relatively low rate, about 5 percent, but the amount repayable is increased by reference to an agreed index, application of which protects the lender from erosion of his capital.

A further benefit from the use of debt is that interest payable could serve to set up a "tax shield," i.e. its payment could reduce the firm's liability to corporate taxation. Although different countries have slightly different tax regulations, interest is generally an allowable deduction when computing the liability to corporate taxation, but dividends are not wholly deductible. Thus, if a company is in a tax paying position, the relief from tax due to the deductibility of interest may substantially reduce the net-of-tax cost of such interest, e.g. a quoted interest rate of 15 percent would cost the borrower only 7½ percent if interest were tax deductible when the tax rate was 50 percent.

The aggregate benefits from gearing, inflation, and taxation appear to make debt financing very attractive indeed, and one is tempted to ask why a firm should not use ever increasing quantities of debt to the ever increasing benefit to shareholders! Unfortunately, all good things must come to an end: many factors serve to restrict either a firm's ability or willingness to use debt financing. Such factors might arise either internally or externally. Let us consider some of these now.

The most significant internal factor arises from the legal documents which regulate the conduct of the company. It is not unusual for such regulatory documents of incorporation to include a clause which limits the amount of borrowing: either in absolute terms or to some proportion of the current amount of issued share capital. Clearly such restrictions must not be exceeded or the company is acting *ultra vires.* If it wishes to borrow more, it should first take steps to amend the offending documents. A further internal constraint could be set up by the nature and availability of corporate assets. If the lender of borrowed capital looks for asset backing of a certain type against which to secure a loan, e.g. real estate, then the company's ability to borrow will be restricted by the absence of such security. Yet another internal constraint could be the attitude of corporate management. Some individuals have an aversion to debt, either for puritanical reasons or from some bitter lesson of the downside risk from the use of debt experienced at an earlier, formative stage in their career; others are naturally conservative or cautious. Corporate policy is frequently a reflection of the personal attitudes of senior management and, thus, if a company has a majority of such individuals at the top, it is likely to adopt a cautious attitude towards the use of debt.

External factors more frequently present the ultimate constraint than do internal factors. Clearly no one can borrow more than the lender will provide. There are a number of rules applied by the lender, some of which often are seen to be no more than apparently illogical rules of thumb because they are based on accepted norms of good practice. It is generally accepted in any environment that it is good to appear to be "normal" but bad to be "abnormal." Therefore, lenders will prefer to be normal but, even if they are not, financial analysts will no doubt comment adversely on the borrower's apparent abnormality and this could be detrimental to the image of the company. Thus, a normal relationship between borrowing and shareholders' capital tends to be established, beyond which it will be difficult for a company to go. Such a norm may vary over time, but certainly varies from industry to industry and from country to country. Thus, shipping tends to have a higher norm for borrowing than textiles due to the nature of the assets which the former is typically able to offer in security. Some countries in continental Europe accept different proportions of debt in their capital structures than does the United Kingdom; Japanese companies, on the other hand, typically experience considerably higher proportions of debt than either European or American companies. Figures 6.4 and 6.5 summarize recent experience. Although the most significant norm is the relationship of debt to shareholders' capital, others will be applied, for example, the asset coverage or the relationship of debt to fixed assets; the earnings coverage or the relationship of EBIT (profit or earnings before interest and tax) to interest payable. Having considered the norm, the lender will also consider whether this can be reason-

	Germany	USA	France	Italy	UK	Japan
GROSS SAVINGS[1]	41.7	55.9	n.a.	33.9	41.7	34.5
CAPITAL TRANSFERS (NET)[2]	11.0	n.a.	n.a.	4.7	5.4	-
TOTAL BORROWING AND OTHER SOURCES: *of which in percentage terms*	47.3	44.1	n.a.	56.2	52.9	65.5
Money market paper and short-term securities	0.6	-0.6	-	-	3.7	-
Short-term (including bank) loans	20.7	25.4	33.6	34.9	60.7	63.2[4]
Shares	2.9	13.0	9.6	18.5	6.7	4.8
Bonds	3.2	15.3	15.4	8.2	5.6	1.3
Long-term bank loans	49.4 }	34.2 }	34.7 }	38.4[3] }	22.4 }	5
Other long-term loans	11.9 }					
Trade credit	-	17.9	5.6	-	1.5	28.9
Other	11.4	-5.3	1.0	-	-	1.8
STATISTICAL ADJUSTMENT	-	-	-	5.2	-	-

n.a. - not available

Notes
[1] Gross savings represents mainly retained earnings and amounts set aside for depreciation.
[2] Capital transfers represents goverment grants and transfers from other sectors of the economy.
[3] Including medium-term loans
[4] Including medium- and long-term loans.
[5] Included with short-term loans.

Figure 6.4 Sources of finance of enterprises (excluding financial institutions) in 1972 (France 1971) in percentage terms (Source: OECD Financial Statistics, Bank of Italy Annual Report—reproduced from Barclays Review, August 1974)

Year	Total	Undistributed income[1]	Bank borrowing[2]	Issues of securities (net)		Capital transfers	Other loans and mortgages[3]	Overseas[4]
				Ordinary shares	Debentures & Pref. shares			
1966	3,837	2,651	187	124	451	26	106	292
1967	4,054	2,684	333	65	350	236	28	358
1968	5,472	3,277	569	299	183	454	121	569
1969	5,793	3,223	664	177	335	598	211	585
1970	5,888	3,002	1,125	39	154	526	306	736
1971	6,388	3,452	730	152	215	595	288	956
1972	9,606	4,571	2,988	317	289	407	141	893
1973	13,624	6,229	4,504	98	51	378	881	1,483
In percentage terms:								
1966	100	69.1	4.9	3.2	11.8	0.7	2.8	7.6
1970	100	51.0	19.1	0.7	2.6	8.9	5.2	12.5
1973	100	45.7	33.1	0.7	0.4	2.8	6.5	10.9

Notes

[1]Before allowing for depreciation, stock appreciation and additions to reserves.
[2]After addition of 40 percent of the excess of debit over credit transit items.
[3]Comprising hire purchase debt, loans from the public sector and loans by financial institutions.
[4]Comprising import and export credit, capital issues overseas, investments by overseas companies, etc.

Figure 6.5 Sources of capital funds of industrial and commercial companies in the UK (in $million) (Source: Central Statistical Office, Financial Statistics and reproduced from Barclays Review (August 1974)

ably applied to the individual borrower. Here the corporate image of the borrower, including his credit status and track record on previous similar occasions, may present a further external constraint: does it all add up to a good or bad risk in the eyes of the potential lender? Finally, some of the factors referred to earlier in this chapter when reviewing the general considerations concerning the selection of an external source of financing, e.g. economic and market environment, fashion, and timing, could represent external constraining influences on the ability of the company to borrow at a particular point in time.

But perhaps the most significant restriction on the use of debt arises from the attendant risks associated with its use. When we were discussing the advantages of gearing, we made reference to the associated downside risk to equity shareholders' earnings should earnings before interest and tax (EBIT) begin to fall. However, there are other potential risks to the shareholder arising from the use of debt. Although the shareholder will normally be happy to see an enhancement in the EPS (earnings per share), the ultimate measure of value comes from the market value of the share and this is the product not only of the earnings per share, but also of the price/earnings multiple (or P/E ratio), *viz:*

$$\text{Market price} = \text{EPS} \times \text{P/E}$$

The graph of Figure 6.3 revealed the volatility of EPS as EBIT moves up or down in differently geared situations. In a highly geared company, the *quality* of EPS could thereby become suspect in the market and this could cause a downgrading in the P/E ratio. Is there any risk that the use of debt, while increasing the EPS might also reduce the P/E ratio? Clearly, there would be no merit in using debt to increase EPS from \$.15/share to \$.20 /share if the P/E were thereby reduced from 6 to 4 because the net effect would be to reduce the market price of an equity share from \$90/share to \$80/share, i.e. from 15 × 6 to 20 × 4. Certainly, the increased use of debt must add an element of risk to equity earnings and, furthermore, the prior interest charge adds an element of doubt to the company's ability to continue to service its equity dividends. Both these factors, *if significant,* must serve to reduce the P/E ratio: but there is no empirical evidence to support with any certainty or predictability by how much it will be reduced. Some theorists argue that because no real *intrinsic* value has been created for the company by the addition of an increment of debt, there can be no real enhancement to shareholder value. Therefore, they further argue that the market price will automatically adjust downward the P/E ratio for each increment of debt so that any enhancement in EPS created by the use of debt will automatically be offset by an appropriate reduction in P/E ratio, thereby maintaining a constant value to equity. Such an argument possesses an undeniable logic; however, to argue thus assumes that the stock market is a completely rational, fully informed, and finely tuned mechanism. But this is not so: experience has frequently revealed that the stock market is none of these things.

In reality, it tends to lurch from one position to another once it is triggered off by the weight of accumulating evidence or by a newly discovered situation. It is in this context that some of the norms referred to above take on a very real, practical significance. Excessively abnormal use of debt will no doubt cause re-assessment of P/E multiples but there must be considerable bands of indifference between one trigger point and the next which the astute financial manager should explore and exploit by utilizing increasing amounts of debt to the advantage of equity shareholder values. The stock market would no doubt react if the use of debt shot up from 5 to 85 percent of total capital overnight, but it is doubtful if it would react violently to a more modest increment. For example, the situation could be as in Figure 6.6—a little debt could be a good thing whereas a lot is clearly bad.

But perhaps the greatest risks to the shareholder created by the use of debt are the risk of the company's inability to maintain payment of a dividend and the risk of complete loss of the investment due to bankruptcy of the company created by the inability to service or repay the debt itself. These are very real risks and are the most important to weigh in the balance when considering how much debt it is wise to carry without unfavorably affecting the real value of equity shareholders' investment. Furthermore, these risks are concerned with the adequacy of cash flow coverage (an internal and personal matter to the company) rather than with earnings or assets coverage which were an important feature of the external norms to which reference was made above. A valid assessment of the debt capacity of a company, i.e. the maximum amount it is considered safe to borrow, therefore, must be closely related to the forecast of future internal cash flows. This is a further reason why a firm should attempt a long-term cash forecast. Once a capital structure has been determined, the company will have to live with it for a number of years. During this time, the capital structure will set up financial obligations which represent contractual cash outflows on servicing the capital, e.g. interest, dividends, lease payments, and on ultimate repayment (unless the whole of the capital is equity). If adverse condi-

Figure 6.6

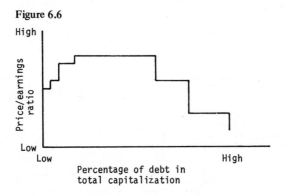

tions should strike the company, will it be able to ride out the storm or will the financial obligations prove too much? There can be either "too much" in an ultimate sense of precipitating bankruptcy; or, short of bankruptcy, too much to permit the company to undertake other cash outflows which are necessary to the continuing health of the company, for example normal replacement capital investments, minimum research, and development expenditures; or too much to keep good faith with its suppliers and so incur an adverse credit rating, perhaps for a long period thereafter.

The impact of variation in earnings on EPS shown in Figure 6.3 can be adapted to reveal similarly the impact of variations in earnings on internally generated cash flow and, thereby, the impact on the firm's ability to meet its contractual cash outflows under different levels of borrowing (see Figure 6.7). The diagonal line represents the internally generated cash flow at different levels of EBIT (notice that even at an EBIT of 0 there is still a positive cash flow due to the incidence of the non-cash depreciation charge). The horizontal lines represent the necessary cash outflows in each of the situations which formed the three companies example used above; these outflows have been computed in Figure 6.8. The diagram reveals that level of EBIT below which the ability to meet all the necessary cash outflows is in doubt: *viz* $400 in situation A; $120 in B; $450 in C, i.e. that point at which either the dividend or the reinvestment must be cut or where recourse must be had to some further source of funds. More importantly, the diagram reveals that level of EBIT below which the ability to continue to meet the debt servicing obligations is in doubt: *viz*—$100 in B; +$50 in C, i.e. that point at which the lender could take legal action to foreclose.

However, this diagram suffers from the disadvantage of being static. It

Figure 6.7 Impact of variation in earnings on ability to meet contractual cash outflows

	Company A $	Company B $	Company C $
Equity capital ($1 shares)	1000	800	500
Debt capital	–	200	500
Total remunerated capital	$1000	$1000	$1000
Interest on debt, say 10% – net cash payement after tax	–	10	25
Repayment of debt, say equal cash instalments over 5 years	–	40	100
Total debt servicing contractual cash outflows	–	50	125
Minimum dividend, 20%	200	160	100
Minimum maintenance reinvestment in fixed assets	100	100	100
Total necessary cash outflows	$300	$310	$325

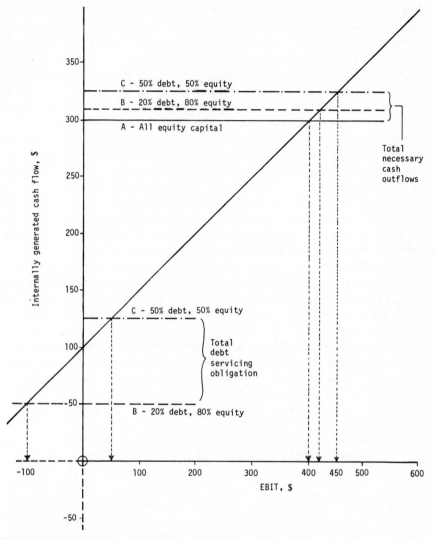

Figure 6.8 Demonstration of the impact of capital gearing, or leverage, on contractual and other necessary cash outflows

is impossible to reflect on such a generalized chart all those variables which affect either the quantity or the timing of internally generated cash flow. For this reason, in practice it would be helpful to project a range of long-term cash forecasts assuming differently geared (or leveraged) capital structures and assuming different combinations and levels of the principal determinants of internally generated cash flow. The object of the exercise would be to reveal under what conditions the company will be exposed to circumstances which could put it at risk due to the adverse behavior of cash flows. Those responsible for determining a debt policy are thus able to assess the potential risks at stake and to determine the degree to which they are prepared to accept those risks and whether they need to ensure against a potentially adverse situation by maintaining appropriate financial reserves. It is important to stress that the choice concerns *degree* of risk: debt does not create a choice between risk and no risk because there is the possibility of an inadequate cash flow precipitating bankruptcy even with an all-equity capital structure. If the decision is taken to go ahead with that capital structure which presents a high risk then the next logical step is to develop contingent action plans which can be implemented should the worst happen. This aspect of financial management's responsibility will be taken up in a later chapter.

Having determined the maximum amount of debt it is wise to incur by considering the internal and external constraints and the risks to liquidity, one question remains: 'How much of this debt capacity should be used?' This may appear to be an odd question because surely the outcome of the analysis just described is to reveal the maximum safe limit to debt and, therefore, this amount certainly should be used up to the hilt. However, this is not necessarily so because a basic rule of any financing decision should be to retain future flexibility. It is not necessarily wise to go up to the hilt on the use of debt in one decision if this thereby prevents a choice and so forces an issue of equity financing in the next round. This could occur just at a time when equity prices are depressed and so be a most inopportune occasion for such an issue. On the other hand, a currently favorable equity price could suggest an equity issue despite the existence of unused debt capacity.

6.7 USE OF PREFERRED STOCK CAPITAL

That part of the capital structure on which dividends are paid is of two types: preferred stock capital and equity or common stock capital. The preferred share typically receives a fixed annual percentage dividend which has a prior call on earnings available for dividend and which must be paid in full before any distribution can be made to equity shareholders. A partial preferred dividend cannot be paid and if there is an insufficiency of earnings in any one year the right to a dividend lapses unless the share is a cumulative preferred share. In this case, any unpaid dividend will be carried forward and all cumulative arrears must first be paid before any dividend can be paid to equity shareholders. The preferred shareholder does not normally have a vote unless the dividend is in arrears. The preferred share may be redeemed at some predetermined future date or dates at par or at a specified premium; should the company go into liquidation the preferred share will be paid this amount in priority to any payment to the ordinary share but after meeting all creditors and other prior claims.

The preferred share is thus in many ways more akin to an unsecured loan than to a share. However, it is legally a share and as such is serviced by dividend, whereas a loan is serviced by interest. The distinction between dividend and interest is not merely academic: we referred above to the fact that interest is tax deductible; on the other hand, a dividend typically is not wholly tax deductible. To a tax-paying company, a 15 percent interest might work out less costly in terms of net cash than a 10 percent preferred dividend. It all depends on the current tax legislation regulating the degree of deductibility of preferred dividend and, of course, the current rates of tax.

Bearing in mind that, on the one hand, the preferred shareholder enjoys few of the benefits of either equity shareholder or debenture holder (neither capital gain, increasing dividend, security, nor voting rights) and, on the other hand, the company enjoys higher tax relief on interest than on dividend, one is tempted to ask "Why issue preferred shares at all?" And, of course, many companies do not. In the United Kingdom, one of the reasons why preferred shares might be issued is when the preferred shareholder is itself a limited company and pays corporation tax. There could then be certain tax advantages to be had by such a shareholder from receipt of preferred dividend rather than debenture interest. Hence, to a pension fund or other institutional investor the preferred share could become an attractive element within its investment portfolio. A further more general reason is that there are limits to the amount of borrowing a company might undertake. If the limit has been reached, due to the obligatory application of some rule of thumb based on the balance sheet relationship between borrowed and shareholder capital or because the company has no appropriate security to offer, then preferred capital could well prove a practical alternative to the issue of new equity capital. In this way, the benefit of fixed return capital is achieved and the diluting effect of new equity shares has been avoided.

6.8 USE OF EQUITY SHARE CAPITAL

Equity shareholders are the ultimate owners of the business, their capital is serviced, if at all, by a dividend but an equity investment offers neither guaranteed return nor security of capital. To the shareholder, the investment, therefore, represents risk capital which enjoys whatever earnings remain after meeting all prior charges. Whatever part of these earnings is not paid in dividend is used within the business, hopefully for further benefit in the future. It is worth re-emphasizing some of the points made earlier in this chapter: the initial cost of raising equity capital is high; equity voting rights control the company; the quantity of shares to be issued to secure a given amount of funds will be determined by the ongoing market value of the share.

For all of these reasons, it is clear that an issue of equity capital should not be undertaken lightly. Furthermore, by raising new equity capital, the company is denying to the equity shareholder any benefits of leverage which would have accrued had other capital been used instead. In addition, any future earnings available for equity must be divided by a greater number of shares. Both these factors lead to an inevitable dilution in EPS (earnings per share), both now and in the future, if new equity shares are issued. If equity capital must be raised, it is the responsibility of financial management to minimize the impact of this inevitable dilution: hence the importance of timing of an issue within the context of fluctuating share prices and also the value of using convertible securities. Convertibles will at least delay the impact of dilution because the future conversion price will be higher than the present share price (thereby reducing the number of shares to be issued). Furthermore, by the time conversion takes place, earnings available for equity should be higher than at the time of issue due to the profitable employment in the meantime of the capital that has been raised.

Equity share capital can be raised either from new shareholders or from existing shareholders. In the latter case, the capital raising may be direct, through the issue of additional shares (a rights issue) or indirect through the retention of earnings otherwise available for dividend. Thus, in this context it can be seen that the dividend decision is inescapably bound up with the financing decision—the lower the dividend, the lower is the amount which must be raised as additional financing and vice versa.

6.9 DEVELOPMENT OF A DIVIDEND POLICY

Let us digress for a moment and consider the factors that might help a firm determine its attitude towards dividend distribution to equity shareholders. If the firm needs additional financing should it simply decide not to pay a dividend? Is the nature of the dividend decision to determine how much of the available earnings to distribute and retain the rest or is it to determine how much to retain and distribute the rest?

The equity dividend decision creates a paradox. If the dividend payout is reduced or eliminated, the intrinsic value of the firm must thereby be increased by the amount of cash retained. Surely, therefore, this should be reflected in an enhanced market value for the equity share. Yet if the dividend is reduced there is a high probability that the market value of the share will actually fall! There can be no rationale for a paradox, but the reason for the dividend paradox would appear to be attributable partly to the inherent irrationality of the stock market and also to the differing degrees of sophistication and differing attitudes and expectations towards receipt of additional cash in the form of dividend within that amorphous mass called equity shareholders. Clearly shareholder expectations must be honored if at all possible, but there would seem to be little merit in distributing more cash than is absolutely necessary to maintain equity share values in the market place. It is a relatively simple matter to canvass the expectation of shareholders in a closely controlled "family" company but it becomes progressively difficult, to the point of impossibility, to do so as the number and type of shareholders (e.g. low tax paying individuals, high tax paying individuals, institutional investors) increases. The large company with a diverse composition of equity shareholders can try to ascertain, or even shape, shareholder expectations through financial public relations work, but generally speaking it must have its dividend policy guided by the attitude and expectation of "the market."

The attitude and expectation of the stock market is difficult to define and there is insufficient evidence to spell out exactly how important a part the dividend plays in the determination of market values. However the following ground rules have emerged:

1 Generally a stable dividend, as opposed to a fluctuating one, is regarded as a sign of strength and, therefore, is likely to have a favorable impact on market value. Indeed, a frequent reason for paying a particular dividend is simply that this was the amount paid last year.

2 Steady, as opposed to erratic, growth is desirable. Dividend growth frequently is allowed to lag slightly behind growth in earnings to emphasize confidence in the new dividend rate. This is preferable to a more immediately sensitive increase giving rise to the need for a subsequent cut in dividend.

3 Dividend cover also plays its part. Dividend cover is the relationship between the maximum earnings available for dividend and the amount actually paid. Although perhaps of less immediate significance, a reasonable cover gives a guide to potential future increases in the amount payable and also indicates the amount of retained earnings which should result in future growth in market value—provided such retention is successfully employed about the business.

4 The stock market does not like shocks. If the unexpected happens, the market tends to read the worst into the situation, predict gloomy prospects, and overreact. A sudden and unexpected cut in dividend, or worse still a broken promise, could have a disastrous effect upon market values. The stock market must be shielded from such shocks and the "information content" of a dividend announcement must be considered very carefully so that the worst is not feared.

A little psychology clearly plays its part in the dividend decision.

Irrespective of the cash dividend that the market expects, that our shareholders wish to receive, or what we can afford to pay, there may be forces at work to restrict dividend distribution. Such forces may arise from:

1 *Contractual obligation,* e.g. a clause in a loan agreement.

2 *Economic restriction:* many companies have been prevented from paying larger, or promised, dividends by dividend restraint forming part of a government's anti-inflation economic package.

3 *Other government intervention,* e.g. by host governments who wish to restrict the repatriation of funds to foreign countries.

Thus, the company is not always a free agent when determining its dividend policy.

Finally, in this brief review of the dividend policy let us consider the role of the stock or scrip dividend. As a means of conserving cash, or due to the imposition of certain restrictions, a company might consider the payment of a scrip dividend, i.e. a dividend representing additional shares rather than an outright cash payment. In theory, the shareholder who prefers cash to scrip may sell at the going market rate and so obtain cash income while maintaining initial capital intact. Thus, the best of both worlds is achieved: the company retains its cash and the shareholder receives what cash he or she desires. However, although possible in theory, in practice it is neither simple nor economic (due to the incidence of transaction costs) to effect the sale of a small parcel of shares. The scrip dividend, therefore, would not normally be seen purely and simply as a corporate cash conservation exercise.

6.10   USE OF "OFF THE BALANCE SHEET" FINANCING

In this chapter, we have been considering the management of long-term financing and this has led us into a review of the spectrum of sources of financing. We have looked at internal sources, the use of "free" capital, the use of borrowed capital, (including a brief excursion into debt policy), the use of preferred share capital, and the use of equity share capital (including a brief excursion into dividend policy). All that has been considered so far has resulted in an entry on the balance sheet but let us now move on to consider those external sources of financing which do not result in any entry on the balance sheet. Examples of such "off the balance sheet" financing are leasing agreements and the factoring of debtors or accounts receivable. In deciding upon an "off the balance sheet" source of financing, an essential first step is to ascertain its cost to the "borrower."

If one had to decide between alternative borrowing opportunities, one factor of considerable importance would be the after-tax cost of interest under each alternative. By the same token, when deciding between financing "on the balance sheet" by borrowing or "off the balance sheet", e.g. by leasing, the after-tax cost of borrowing, i.e. interest, should be compared to the after-tax cost of leasing, i.e. the implied interest element incorporated into the leasing package. In a lease, the lessor is putting his or her own funds into the venture and is not going to do it gratuitously. Irrespective of whether the "loan" is legally called lending or leasing, the lessor is looking for a rate of return and that rate of return is presumably the cost to us. But how does one set about ascertaining this implied interest cost? In fact, it is a relatively straightforward exercise provided one can isolate the cash flows set up purely by the decision to lease; such cash flows will naturally depend on the specific terms of the leasing agreement but in general will embrace the following:

1   The cash outflow on future rental payments.

2   A reduction in future cash outflows on taxation due to the tax deductibility of future rental payments.

3   Any change in future cash flow created by the legal shift in ownership when comparing leasing with outright purchase, e.g. the loss of terminal values or the increase in future cash outflows on taxation due to the loss of taxation depreciation allowances.

4   Any other change in future cash flow created by the leasing package, e.g. a reduction in future cash outflows arising from maintenance work or any other service undertaken by the lessor on behalf of the lessee.

5   Changes in future cash outflows on taxation consequent upon changes in taxable or tax deductible items arising at (4) above.

Note that these cash flows are those arising purely from *leasing* and not from *operating* the asset being leased.

The cash flows that have thus been isolated represent to the lessor the recovery of capital (sunk into the capital value of the asset being leased) together with interest representing a compound rate of return on however much of the capital that remains unrecovered for as long as it remains unrecovered. And, of course, this is exactly what is implied in the cash flows associated with a more formal "on the balance sheet" loan. The compound rate of return incorporated into any such pattern of future cash flows can be ascertained quite simply by application of a technique from the discounted cash flow family which bears the title "internal rate of return."

Having ascertained in this way the true after-tax cost of leasing, it can now be compared to the after-tax cost of borrowing although the ultimate decision would not normally be taken on the basis of cost alone. There are other factors to weigh in the balance when considering the lease as a source of financing, for example:

1 Some of the risks associated with ownership, e.g. breakdown and obsolescence, might be avoided by leasing and any extra cost might be considered a modest premium to pay for such avoidance.

2 The future pattern of cash flows under leasing is quite predictable and spread smoothly over a number of years. Therefore, it might be more easily accommodated within the cash forecast than the pattern of cash flows associated with a debt and ownership alternative.

3 The leasing agreement in effect permits 100 percent borrowing against the cost of the asset acquired. Very few debt alternatives would permit this.

4 The very fact that the lease is "off the balance sheet" might permit the firm to obtain finance beyond its externally computed debt capacity and without risk to its credit rating. In theory this should not be possible but in practice credit analysts might overlook this supplemental source of finance when computing some of the traditional balance sheet ratios that underlie accepted norms of good practice.

6.11 DISCOUNTED CASH FLOWS

There are two broad types of discounted cash flow methods for capital budgeting:

1 Internal rate of return ("IRR method").

2 Net present value ("NPV method").

Both of these methods discount the stream of future cash flows resulting from a capital investment, unlike the simpler "payback method" and the "rate of return on average investment" (or "average rate of return").

Discounting is the opposite of compounding. Thus, with compounding the movement is from the present to the future, e.g. if the annual compound rate of interest is 10 percent, you know that $1 today will be worth $1.10 in one year from now. Discounting will, therefore, tell you that $1.10 discounted at 10 percent is the present value of $1 for a one year period. The term "present value" indicates a movement from the future back to the present.

A capital investment, e.g. an investment in a factory or machinery, is expected to bring in future cash flows, but there is a waiting period. It is, therefore, necessary to take into account the cost of waiting. This is also known as the "time value of money." The waiting period can be 1 year, 2 years, 3 years, or any amount of time. Discounting will tell you the loss in value for waiting.

6.12 PRESENT VALUE

$$\text{Present Value of \$1 after n number of years} = \frac{\$1}{(1+r)^n}$$

$$\text{Present Value of \$1 after 1 year} = \frac{\$1}{1+10\%} = \frac{\$1}{1.10} = \$0.90909$$

$$\text{Present Value of \$1 after 2 years} = \frac{\$1}{(1+10\%)^2} = \frac{\$1}{(1.10)^2} = \$0.82645$$

$$\text{Present Value of \$1 after 3 years} = \frac{\$1}{(1+10\%)^3} = \frac{\$1}{(1.10)^3} = \$0.75131$$

$$\text{Present Value of \$1 after 4 years} = \frac{\$1}{(1+10\%)^4} = \frac{\$1}{(1.10)^4} = \$0.68301$$

Total Present Value $3,16986
where r = 10 percent

In the above calculations, 10 percent would be a company's required rate of return for making an investment, for example, engaging in a project, buying a machine, or building a new factory.

6.13 INTERNAL RATE OF RETURN

The internal rate of return is computed as follows:

$$I_0 = \frac{CI_1}{1+r} + \frac{CI_2}{(1+r)^2} + \frac{CI_3}{(1+r)^3} + \dots + \frac{CI^n}{(1+r)^n}$$

where I_0 = original investment
           (i.e., cash outflow)
   CI_1 = cash inflow for the first year
   CI_2 = cash inflow for the second year
   CI_3 = cash inflow for the third year
   CI_n = cash inflow for the last year
     n = the last year for which there is a cash inflow
     r = internal rate of return

For example, if you are given the following data

$$I_0 \ = \$100,000$$
$$CI_1 = \$\ \ 31,547.13$$
$$CI_2 = \$\ \ 31,547.13$$
$$CI_3 = \$\ \ 31,547.13$$
$$CI_4 = \$\ \ 31,547.13$$

the formula for calculating the internal rate of return is:

$$\$100,000 = \frac{\$31,547.13}{1+r} + \frac{\$31,547.13}{(1+r)^2} + \frac{\$31,547.13}{(1+r)^3} + \frac{\$31,547.13}{(1+r)^4}$$

What you now have to determine, in order to solve for r, is the discount factor which when multiplied by $31,547.13 equals the original investment of $100,000.

The discount factor is computed as follows:

$$\frac{\$100,000}{\$31,547.13} = 3.16986$$

This discount factor tells us that r = 10 percent. This was already calculated (see under Section 6.12 "PRESENT VALUE").

In a more general form, the cash outlay for an investment divided by the cash inflow per year yields the discount factor. One need merely look at a present value table (which can be found in many finance books) for a uniform series under the number of years involved to get the amount of the cash inflow and find that particular discount factor. The table will then give the percentage rate of return directly (or it can be obtained by interpolation, if the exact amount is not given in the table).

6.14 NET PRESENT VALUE

In contrast to the internal rate of return, net present value is calculated as follows:

Net Present Value = −Original Investment (cash outflow)
+ Present Value of the Discounted Cash Inflows

Thus, using the same figures as before:

$$\text{Net Present Value} = -\$100,000 + \frac{\$31,547.13}{1.10} + \frac{\$31,547.13}{(1.10)^2} + \frac{\$31,547.13}{(1.10)^3}$$

$$+ \frac{\$31,547.13}{(1.10)^4}$$

$$= -\$100,000 + \$100,000 = 0$$

Conclusion: investment can be accepted.

The above answer is zero. This means the investment can be accepted. If the answer had been a negative number, then that would mean that the investment should not be accepted. Any positive number would make the investment acceptable and the larger the positive number, the more acceptable the investment. For example:

$$\text{Net Present Value} = -\$100,000 + \frac{\$30,000}{1.10} + \frac{\$30,000}{(1.10)^2} + \frac{\$30,000}{(1.10)^3} + \frac{\$30,000}{(1.10)^4}$$

$$= -\$100,000 + \$95,096 = -\$4,904$$

Conclusion: investment should be rejected.

$$\text{Net Present Value} = -\$100,000 + \frac{\$40,000}{1.10} + \frac{\$40,000}{(1.10)^2} + \frac{\$40,000}{(1.10)^3} + \frac{\$40,000}{(1.10)^4}$$

$$= -\$100,000 + \$126,795 = +\$26,795$$

Conclusion: investment can be accepted.

6.15 CAPITAL STRUCTURE DECISION

Let us pause at this stage, before finally going on to consider some more specialized sources of financing, to recapitulate and summarize those matters which the wise financial manager will consider when determining the most appropriate mix of normal domestic external sources of funds. The financing decision is taken after considering many complex and often conflicting facts, opinions, and viewpoints. Thus, it is difficult to encapsulate the decision in a few words but, even so, the following decision rule is suggested regarding a firm's capital structure:

1 *"Free capital"*—Take the maximum amount legally permissible, having first confirmed that it bears no implied cost that is, in fact, higher than the cheapest available alternative.

2 *Borrowed capital*—Use the maximum amount that future flexibility and internal or external constraints permit provided that it can be employed in the firm at a continuing rate of return in excess of its cost and provided that it does not detract from the value of equity nor endanger the continuity of the firm due to the increased risks thereby assumed.

3 *Preferred capital*—Use only if there are valid reasons, either now or anticipated to make this more attractive than borrowed capital.

4 *Equity capital*—Use when it is considered inadvisable to use other sources or because other sources might not otherwise be made available in the future and use in such a way as to minimize dilution to present and future earnings and values per equity share.

5 *Leasing*—Use only if the cost is lower than the cheapest available alternative or if there are valid advantages to be gained which would not otherwise be available.

Notice reference in this summary to the need to maintain future flexibility. It is a wise basic management decision rule that as far as possible no decision should be taken today which will deny freedom of choice in the future. This also holds true for the financing decision: future options must be kept open.

6.16 SPECIAL DOMESTIC SOURCES OF FINANCING

In addition to the normal external domestic sources of financing which we have reviewed, there are other sources which might arise under certain peculiar circumstances. Most important in this context is the assistance which is frequently given by governments, of whatever nationality, to encourage investment in certain underdeveloped areas. Such assistance becomes available at certain times and under certain conditions as the government's current economic policy dictates. Normally such financial assistance is provided on apparently very favorable terms. However, a firm seeking such financing should seriously consider any potential financial or nonfinancial disadvantages associated with operating in that area to which government assistance induced them to move. Such disadvantages might represent a substantial future hidden cost of obtaining this particular source of finance.

Financial burdens can be eased considerably if they are shared with others. A further potential source of finance is thus a joint venture or other arrangement with another enterprise.

Finally, let us not overlook the possible source of financing created by merger or takeover. If one firm so badly mismanages its control and utilization of cash it could present a highly favorable takeover prospect to another, better managed firm that will unlock the cash flow potential which has been allowed to lie fallow by the erring management. Inefficient cash management by one presents an open invitation for another to come along and attempt to pick up what is seen to be a relatively inexpensive source of badly needed funds.

6.17 FINANCING FOREIGN OPERATIONS

The mechanics of short- and long-term cash forecasting for a foreign operation are basically similar to those already described for a domestic operation; the sources of funds available to the foreign operation are also similar to those available to the domestic operation. However there are certain differences, in particular:

1 A decision has to be taken on the amount of financing which will be raised locally in the foreign country and the amount which will be provided by the domestic parent.

2 The parent must consider the management of its resources on a worldwide basis, hopefully in such a way as to minimize international tax liabilities, international interest costs, and international exchange and other risks, e.g. inflation, government intervention, and restriction or expropriation.

3 Decision rules must be established regarding the location of cash balances internationally and as to the method, e.g. loans, dividends, and transfer price adjustments, and route and timing of international cash transfers.

None of this is easy because the system is overlaid with problems created by living simultaneously with several governments while attempting to avoid the accusation of failing to behave as an honest guest in a host country.

The management of financing in a foreign operation might follow this sequence of steps:

1 *Determine the total cash requirement of the foreign operation:* this implies the stage-by-stage approach to long-term cash forecasting suggested in Chapter 5, but already there are elements of foreign financial policy creeping in because in arriving at this amount the inter-company transfer pricing and remittance policy of the group will have been incorporated.

2 *Determine the amount and type of local external financing:* the principal area for decision concerns the degree to which local nationals shall be given control over the operation and perhaps the determination of future financial policies. Government edict frequently is very strong in this respect.

3 *Determine the type of any necessary nonlocal financing:* provided that there are no home government restrictions on the exporting of money, this step represents the final balancing of the operation, i.e. the amount required to plug the gap between the first two steps. The parent must decide whether such necessary financing should be provided directly from the parent or instead from other currently ongoing foreign operations. Most importantly, the parent must decide how the financing shall be provided. To the obvious selection between debt, preferred and equity capital must be added the further options of inter-company current account or the manipulation of charges and transfer prices for goods and services provided. Also, the facility with which repatriation of the money can be arranged in case of need is clearly an important consideration.

Financing a foreign operation must be approached with considerable care and forethought: not only is the provider of funds exposing itself to the normal operational and financial risks associated with domestic financing operations, it is adding the further dimensions of geographical distance, international exchange fluctuations, and government intervention both at home and abroad.

A particularly interesting case of employing many forms of financing very effectively for operational and financial purposes, both domestic and foreign, is that of Itel Corporation. Itel has made use of common stock and preferred stock offerings, private placements, Eurodebt, and a public offering of debt plus stock (see "Itel's fantastic borrowing coup," *Business Week,* August 28, 1978, pp. 92–93).

Wenman Plastics:
Part 6

This is the final part of the case study. Readers are invited first to review the earlier parts of the case and in particular their views in response to Questions 8, 9, and 10 (Part 5).

Claude and Karl Wenman met on Sunday morning to review Karl's cash forecast (reproduced as Exhibit 8 to Part 5) and to discuss its implications for the future of Wenman Plastics. Both were pleased because it appeared that, if all went well, the company would be able to 'get out of the red' by 1979. On the other hand, both had misgivings:

1 Karl was unsure that all this growth was really necessary. After all he had developed a comfortable existence in the company in a small, quiet way over the past decade. He was adamant that no outside shareholders should be admitted to the company. Moreover, he was worried at the prospect of getting so heavily into debt, remembering that it was the onset of financial difficulties in one of his major customers that had led him into the plastics industry and to the formation of Wenman Plastics Limited in the first place.

181

2   Claude was becoming impatient with his father's lack of enthusiasm and felt that his attitude towards additional shareholders coupled with his insistence on maintaining the dividend was acting as a restraint on the firm's operational flexibility. On the other hand, he realized the considerable risk that Wenman Plastics faced with a broad-scale launch. All the problems that he had thought about the night before (and summarized in Part 4) were fresh in his mind and he realized that there would be little margin for safety once the plan had been put into operation:

a.   there would be little security left for any further borrowing;

b.   instant reserves of investment and cash would have been used up;

c.   inventory policy created very little potential for reduction of inventory levels;

d.   reductions in expense levels would prevent maintenance of the market policy;

e.   the possible extension of credit from suppliers was perhaps the only potential reserve of any value.

Karl and Claude eventually agreed that at least there would be nothing lost in discussing the matter with Mr. Phillips, their bank manager, and so, Claude's forecasts having been submitted in advance, a meeting was arranged later that week.

The meeting with Mr. Phillips proved to be very helpful. Also present at the meeting was a representative of the bank's regional investigation staff.

The bank regarded Wenman Plastics as a valued customer. Its profit record had been good and, in March 1973, its liquid position was excellent. Clearly, if all went well, medium-term financing was all that was required and this represented acceptable business for the bank. However, Mr. Phillips urged a more cautious approach than the broad-scale introduction proposed by Claude Wenman. He recommended that the Wenmans move a little more slowly until sales became more assured, particularly in view of the attendant capital expenditures that were quite out of proportion to the existing position at March 1973. Karl nodded wisely at this suggestion.

Nevertheless, subject to greater assurances on the existence of the market, Mr. Phillips was prepared to undertake the following financing package with Wenman Plastics:

1   Instead of the proposed finance house loan, the bank would offer a seven year $400,000 loan on security of the property with a two year "holiday" on repayments.

2   Additionally, an overdraft facility with an upper limit of $1 million secured by a floating charge on all the assets of Wenman Plastics would be offered.

3   Mr. Phillips undertook to investigate an alternative to (2) elsewhere within the banking group which would involve the purchase of the equipment on hire

purchase over three years thus restructuring the cash flows and reducing the amount required as overdraft facility.

4 The bank would stipulate that no dividends should be paid without the bank's prior agreement while the loan remained unpaid.

Postscript

Claude made further investigations into the market potential and was fortunate to secure firm orders from three major customers which covered a period of six months and guaranteed some 30 percent of his initial capacity. Moreover, possession of the orders allowed Claude to modify his production and inventory policies slightly but advantageously as far as cash flow was concerned. Karl reluctantly agreed to suspend the dividend, Mr. Phillips arranged appropriate financial assistance, and the project went ahead.

Ironically, the major problem faced by Wenman Plastics late in 1973 had not been foreseen by Claude, Karl, or Mr. Phillips. This was the crisis created by the Arab oil producing countries. The dramatic increase in the price of oil at this time quickly affected the raw material prices to Wenman Plastics (in addition to the more general rise in fuel prices) and, thereby, not only affected the firm's cost structure and inventory values but more importantly its whole pattern of cash flows.

7

Reliability
of Forecasts

Perhaps the only thing that can be said with certainty
about a forecast is that it is likely to be wrong
(unless of course the forecaster is clairvoyant!).
This is a fact of life with which we must live
but it need not detract from the value of the forecast. In this chapter,
we turn our attention to uncertainty in forecasting.
We shall suggest that an attempt be made
to quantify the uncertainty, that we clarify
whether or not the uncertainty is critical to the firm,
and that we take appropriate steps to live with it if we have to.
Our brief review of the subject will lead us
into the realms of sensitivity and analysis
and to the great contribution that the computer model can give
in this area of forecasting.

7.1 UNCERTAINTY AND FORECASTS

Uncertainty and forecasting are inseparable. If there were no uncertainty then there would be no need for forecasts: all that would be necessary to plan for future occurrences would be log the outcome of the certain future. The future is by no means certain and indeed the further a forecast pushes into the future, the greater is the degree of uncertainty surrounding the quantitites produced. Regrettably, this is occasionally used as an argument against attempting a forecast, yet, on the contrary, the greater the degree of uncertainty, perhaps the greater is the need for management guidance and, hence, the greater is the need for planning and so for preparing a forecast. Uncertainty is a fact of life with which management must learn to live; similarly management must learn to plan despite uncertainty.

One of the basic problems to be overcome is the naive belief that a forecast which turns out to be "wrong" was a "bad" forecast. Let us be honest: there is a high probability that the forecast will be wrong in that it will not be 100 percent correct in predicting the future. But a "good" forecast is not necessarily the one which, in retrospect, turns out to have been "correct" rather than "wrong." This is not the object of forecasting. A "good" forecast is the one which guides appropriate and timely management action in the changing world and allows comparison between forecast and actual results: this is the object of forecasting. In fact, the *process of forecasting* is often of much greater value to management than the *forecast* itself. The *process* should sharpen management's awareness and, thereby, should initiate more rational management action in response to the changing management environment that develops.

So let us be honest: the future *is* unpredictable and we must live with this fact but still it is wise to undertake the task of both short- and long-term cash forecasting. A forecast indicates what the future *could* be, not what it *will* be.

7.2 SINGLE POINT ESTIMATES

Perhaps one reason why some forecasts are not as helpful to management as they might be is that they are presented as single point estimates and, thereby, convey a spurious air of accuracy, for example: "the sales next year will bring $X thousand into this division." Did the manager who made that forecast really *believe* that the sales would be $X thousand and could not possibly be some other number higher or lower than X? A single point estimate represents the best, albeit subjective, judgment by an individual manager as to what is thought to be the most likely to occur . . . but it can only be right or wrong in actuality (and there is a high probability that it will be wrong!). Forecasting based on single point estimates frequently is a very difficult time for managers, because they must "stick their necks out" and produce a number in the face of considerable doubt. Managers know that up to the planning horizon there will be many uncontrollable events which can prevent the forecast from being achieved. But ultimately, managers must come to terms with the uncertainty that surrounds their decision, resolve their doubts, and make up their mind. They, thus, produce a number which will be fed into the forecasting system. Ironically, after producing this number they will frequently argue its merit or viability as if there had been at the time no uncertainty at all! Yet how scientific was the resolution of these doubts?

In practice, the manner in which the doubts were resolved may have been considerably colored by the psychology of the circumstances surrounding the preparation of the estimate. Advice will have been sought but the weight of such "advice" varies depending upon whether it was given by an independent advisor, a service department within the firm, a subordinate, a peer, or a superior. Moreover, the answer which the manager knows is expected by his superior or by the "system" will occasionally color the manner in which uncertainty is resolved.

Now the typical forecasting process will combine many individual estimates from many individual managers at different levels in the organizational structure. Many other numbers will then be produced as part of the process based upon the estimates which have been fed into the forecasting system. Unfortunately, when several single point estimates—culled from various managers—are put together, they could produce a combined final net forecast which is in fact most *un*likely to occur. The tragedy is that subsequent decisions based on such forecasts might be taken in complete ignorance of the very doubts that existed in the minds of those who, at an earlier stage and perhaps at a different point in the organizational structure, produced the estimates which formed the basis for the forecast. Such doubts may or may not be material to the subsequent decision but, had they been kept alive within the forecasting system instead of having been eliminated at the individual estimate stage, then that subsequent decision could perhaps have represented the outcome of much more reasoned judgment.

It would seem to be more realistic, and surely more helpful in guiding management action, if all concerned avoid assuming the false accuracy implied by a single point estimate and acknowledge instead that there are margins of doubt or uncertainty in all estimates which individual managers have produced. If the individual manager who is called upon to make an estimate is encouraged to bring uncertainty into the open, by consciously considering not only what is hoped will happen but also what could go wrong, he or she could perhaps produce a range of possible outcomes around the single point best guess estimate which better reflects what is most likely to occur. A minimum three point estimated range (original best guess, plus an anticipated most favorable topside and least favorable bottomside estimated outcome) is surely more helpful than a single point selection from within that range. So why not feed the individual manager's doubts and uncertainty into the forecasting system in the form of an estimated range rather than a single point estimate? Moreover, there must be a greater probability that an estimated range will turn out to be "correct," i.e. that the actual outcome will lie within that range, than will a single point estimate.

7.3 SENSITIVITY ANALYSIS

If the manager is permitted to produce a range of possible outcomes in response to the request for an estimate this will also reduce the worry, to which we have referred, in the mind of the manager who must produce the estimate. Such worry is created by nagging doubts over "What if . . .?" "What if this happens?" or "What if that happens?" implying "Should I say this or should I say that?" But a range may reveal that the outcome will be favorable even if the worst does happen, in which case there is no need to worry at all! On the other hand, the range may reveal that even if the most favorable estimate comes to pass the outcome will still be unfavorable. In this case, there is no real cause to worry either because the indication clearly is that this course of action should not be embarked upon unless it is impossible to avoid doing so.

The problem area is clearly the one where the most favorable estimate produces a favorable outcome but the least favorable estimate produces an unfavorable outcome. In this case, there is indeed the greatest need to worry because if the least favorable, bottomside estimate should come to pass then the firm could be in trouble. Therefore, part of the process of forecasting must be to highlight any such extremely critical or "sensitive" areas by seeking to answer a series of "What if . . .?" questions, e.g. "What will happen to profitability and to liquidity if sales fall by 25 percent?" "What if customers take three months to pay their accounts instead of one month?" "What if interest rates rise to 19 percent?" "What if the rate of inflation reaches 35 percent per annum?" And so on. This aspect of forecasting is called "sensitivity analysis."

The object of sensitivity analysis, by iterative combination of all possible outcomes within the range of estimates submitted, is to isolate within the forecast those critical factors, or key variables, which are likely to have the most critical impact upon the financial fortunes of the firm. Management attention must then be focused on these key variables because they are the killer areas— areas where it is worth seeking more information in order to improve the quality of the best guess estimate; areas where some form of insurance might be sought; areas where subsequent vigilance in the monitoring both of forecasting assumptions and of actual cash flows must be strongest in order to give the earliest warning of an impending financial crisis.

It must be stressed that sensitivity analysis is a relatively simple and unsophisticated concept. All it implies is that several forecasts are produced from a range of estimates fed into the process instead of producing one forecast from single point estimates. The firm is thereby more capable of ascertaining under what combination of circumstances it might be exposed to risks which it would prefer not to face. At best, these risks might represent a break in the continuity of cash flows so as to frustrate certain management decisions considered to be essential to the firm; at worst, they might represent insolvency.

In the preceding chapter, we reviewed the factors that must be taken into account in determining the amount of debt it is considered wise for a firm to take on. Reference was made at that time to the need to ensure that additional debt did not put the future of the firm in jeopardy and a chart representing a static analysis of cash flow coverage was suggested in Figure 6.8. It will now be clear that a more dynamic sensitivity analysis will greatly assist the debt financing decision because thereby management can ascertain, given different combinations of bottomside range estimates, whether there will still be adequate operating cash profile to cover the additional financial obligations taken on with the extra parcel of debt. The "What if . . .?" type question which sensitivity analysis will seek to answer in this context is "Can the firm continue to service its debt obligations out of cash flow under any anticipated recessionary conditions?"

7.4 FINANCIAL MODELS

But let us now be realistic! It is no mean administrative feat to produce one long-term cash forecast, let alone the multiplicity of forecasts required for an acceptable sensitivity analysis. Even if we restrict managers to a simple three point estimate (least favorable, best guess, and most favorable) of the critical key variables, this will still represent a large quantity of combinations. Many finance people have thrown up their hands in horror at the prospect of a revision to the set of plans and have visibly quaked at the suggestion of yet a further revision—so many numbers are interrelated and require amendment. For example, one alteration to sales income in any plan will also cause an alteration to: variable costs, such as direct labor and direct material; all the various stages of profit right down from earnings before interest and tax to earnings retained; debtors or receivables and collections from debtors; perhaps inventories; cash or bank balances . . . at a minimum. There must be a practical limit to the amount of sensitivity analysis that can be undertaken manually. In fact, it is reasonable to ask whether sensitivity analysis is a practical possibility or whether it is just an academic's dream.

Clearly the answer lies in the availability of rapid computational assistance to handle the multiplicity of calculations and iterative tests involved. Fortunately, there is virtually no limit to the amount of analysis that can be tackled by a computer and one very useful management technique which has been developed, largely through the application of computers, is the financial model. Sensitivity analysis is considerably facilitated if a computer model is available. The concept of models is not new. All of us in our younger days played with a baby carriage or a toy train—these are physical models from which we can learn something of the behavior of the real life object upon which it is modeled. It is a short step to symbolic models from which we hope also to learn something of the behavior about the real object upon which it has been modeled. The breakeven chart, the Gantt chart, and the decision tree are examples of graphical simulations, or models, of specific aspects of business life. Similarly, the financial model sets out to help us learn something of the behavior, in financial terms, of all or part of the firm if given changes occur in certain key variables. The output of the financial model would typically be presented in the form of forecast balance sheet, forecast profit statement, and forecast of cash requirements.

The model itself, which is programmed into the computer, is simply an expression of the mathematical relationship that exists between all the given variables. For example, a simple relationship is that a product's sales income equals the quantity sold times the unit selling price: a generalized relationship is that earnings after tax equals X percent of earnings before tax; a more complex relationship would demonstrate that the total cash requirement is the end result of many interacting variables. In fact, it is the end result of all of the items forming lines 1 to 14 of the long-term forecast reproduced in Figure 5.2. In the operation of a model, some of the variables are basic numbers which will be given to the model but others are computed by the model itself from the interaction of two or more other given basic numbers. The grossly oversimplified example in Figure 7.1 demonstrates the operation of a profit statement model. Clearly, the quantity and complexity of calculations rapidly escalates and it is for this reason that financial models can only be of full value to management if they possess the attribute of speed which can only be provided by a computer. Given this speed and simplicity in operation, once the model has been built, management is in the position of being able to interrogate the computer and ascertain the financial consequences of any number of "What if . . .?" questions. In this way, the quality, ease, and speed of strategic and tactical management decisions should be improved.

Perhaps it ought to be stressed that the "What if . . .?" questions are asked, not out of idle curiosity, but to safeguard some critical factor—for example, the ability to pay a dividend. For this reason, it seems logical to develop the use of

Figure 7.1   Simplified profit statement model relationships

Line	Item	Sample instruction
1	Sales	$500,000 (given)
2	Material and related cost	30% line 1
3	Labor and related cost	25% line 1
4	Contribution	Line 1 - lines (2 + 3)
5	Production overhead	$30,000 (given) + 3% line 1
6	Administrative overhead	$50,000 (given)
7	Selling and distribution overhead	$25,000 (given) + 6% line 1
8	Cash flow from operations	Line 4 - lines (5 + 6 + 7)
9	Depreciation	20% plant and machinery balance[1] + 2% buildings balance[1]
10	EBIT (Earnings before interest and tax)	Line 8 - line 9
11	Interest	$5000 (given[2]) + 12% bank overdraft[1]
12	EBT (earnings before tax)	Line 10 - line 11
13	Tax	50% line 12 if positive
14	EAT (Earnings after tax)	Line 12 - line 13
15	Dividend	Lower of 10% equity capital[1] or 50% line 14
16	ERt (Earnings retained)	Line 14 - line 15

[1] These items would be cross-referenced to line numbers in the balance sheet model.
[2] The existing obligation to debenture interest.

sensitivity analysis and financial models by standing the "What if . . .?" question on its head. For example: not "What would be the effect on our ability to pay a dividend if sales fell by X percent?" but "By how much must sales fall before our ability to pay a dividend is placed in jeopardy?" The financial model is also a useful vehicle for testing both the viability of various possible financial strategies and the compatability of various operating and financial strategies. Whereas the computer is not essential to such exercises, it is of course desirable in that it enables more tests to be applied than could possibly be applied manually.

The acceptance and use of computer based financial models has increased dramatically through the late 1960s and early 1970s. This is partially due to an increasing faith in computer applications but considerable impetus has been given to the concept by the relative decline in the cost of computer power, the availability of computer packages, much simpler programming systems and languages, and the growth in use of terminals which permit management "conversational" access to their computer or bureau. The vital answers to management's "What if . . . . . .?" questions should be available within minutes by computer compared to the hours which would no doubt be necessary by manual methods. However, it must be made clear that the computer is by no means essential to sensitivity analysis. It is certainly very helpful in that it permits management to undertake many more sensitivity tests than could possibly be contemplated by manual methods, but even a few manual tests are better than none at all.

Sensitivity analysis concentrates management's attention on those combinations of possible events which could prove critical to the firm's cash position. If the worst combination presents a position that is unacceptable, management must next decide whether it is prepared to live with that risk and this begs the next and most critical question, "What are the changes that the worst combination will come about?"

7.5 QUANTIFYING RISK AND UNCERTAINTY

In the same way that management must learn to live with uncertainty, management must also attempt to *keep it within bounds.* If the result of a piece of sensitivity analysis demonstrates that the bottomside outcome of the range could prove disastrous to the firm, it is surely logical to attempt to assess whether there is a good chance, a fair chance, or a very slim chance that it will happen. Clearly, the greater the chance of its occurrence, the greater is the risk faced by management. In recent years, a branch of management science and decision theory that draws heavily upon the mathematics of probability has seen greater application throughout industry in the quest for an acceptable basis for guiding management decisions in the face of risk and uncertainty. Unfortunately, many managers have little taste for mathematics and tend to be highly skeptical, so let us get the mathematical technique in perspective. No amount of management science will make the decision—that must be management's responsibility— but the quality of a fully informed decision must be greater than an ill informed one. No manager can afford the luxury of overlooking the benefits of logical analysis before reaching his decision. So let us take only a brief look at the mathematics of probability and its application in management decision making. A full exposition on the whole spectrum of management science techniques designed to assist the quantification of risk and uncertainty must be put beyond the scope of this book.

Probability is simply a factor between 0 (indicating no chance at all) and 1.0 (indicating complete certainty). There is a probability of (almost!) 1.0 that the following page in this book will bear the number 193, there is a probability of 0 that the year after next will be 1872. If there are alternative outcomes to an event, the probabilities ascribed to each alternative must add up to 1.0 as there can be nothing greater than certainty. If I flip a coin there can be only two alternative outcomes (assuming that the coin is unbiased and that it does not stand on end as it falls!), each with an equal chance—therefore, there is a 0.5 probability that it will come down heads and a 0.5 probability that it will come down tails; on a single roll of an unloaded die, there must be a probability of 1/6 or 0.1666 that any one number will come up. The example of the coin and the die represent classical probabilities that are easily computed. A further category of probabilities is the statistical or historical probability which puts a size to the probability of an occurrence based upon vast quantities of historical data. Insurance companies bear testimony to the fact that, given a sufficiently large volume or range of business, or spread, there is profit to be made from statistical probability!

'. . .whereas the computer is not essential to such exercises it is or course desirable in that it enables more tests to be applied than could possibly be applied manually. . .

	Course of Action	
	A	B

1 His best guess estimate is
  - therefore the decision would appear to
   be indifferent to either A or B
	+$100	+$100

2 But the most favorable outcome could be
  and the least favorable could be
  - therefore the decision is no longer
   indifferent due to the range of
   possible outcomes and particularly the
   bottom side risk of A
	+$150
	- $80
		+$120
		Zero

3 The probabilities of occurrence are
  thought to be:
    Most favorable
    Best guess
    Least favorable
	
	0.30
	0.60
	0.10
		
		0.25
		0.50
		0.25

	1.00	1.00

4 And the weighted probability
outcome is thus:
```
   For A          +150 x 0.30 = +45
                  +100 x 0.60 = +60
                  - 80 x 0.10 = - 8
                                -----
                                +$97
                                =====

   For B          +120 x 0.25 = +30
                  +100 x 0.50 = +50
                  Zero x 0.25 =   0
                                -----
                                +$80
                                =====
```
  - therefore the decision would favor Course A since +$97 is
   bigger than +$80.

Figure 7.2

But what has all this got to do with management? Here we move into a further category of probabilities: subjective probability (or "gut-feel"!). It is argued that when managers have been asked to forecast a range of possible outcomes and the future proves to be sensitive to that range, they should then indicate their subjective judgment as to scale and sequential nature of many of these, it is also clear that a considerable number of calculations must be undertaken before the final result is known. Therefore, once again the computer is of great assistance in undertaking this sort of analysis. It should also be clear that the ultimate progression is to link sensitivity analysis to the quantification of risk and uncertainty by extending the list of "What if . . .?" questions such as "What if the probabilities are this and not that?" Or, standing sensitivity analysis on its head as suggested in the preceding section, "How low does the probability need to fall before . . .?"

The point was made in Section 7.3 that sensitivity analysis is a relatively simple and unsophisticated concept yet it yields considerable advantages to the manager and so it should be worth applying to aid the preparation of a cash forecast. On the other hand, the subsequent application of mathematical techniques is relatively more expensive, complex, and sophisticated and would no doubt only be applied to the occasionally large, critical decision where the answer is not obvious and where the bottomside risk could be extremely critical to the firm.

7.6 TAKING THE RISK

Having done all the calculations and produced all the mathematically correct answers, someone has got to make the decision. In the example developed in the preceding section, the weighted probability outcome indicated that A (with a weighted probability outcome of +$97) was a better bet than B (with a weighted probability outcome of +$80); but the fact remains that A has a bottomside cash flow of -$80, while B has only zero. If the firm could not afford to lose $80 it would presumably be wise to opt for B despite its lower weighted probability outcome. However, this discussion is in danger of taking us further down the path of mathematical techniques into areas bearing exotic titles such as "utility theory" and "certainty equivalent" so we will go no further. There are many excellent texts to assist the reader who wishes to continue along this path.

However, in a very practical sense, the production of an estimated range and the subsequent development of sensitivity analysis will highlight the potential bottomside risk to the firm. Is the firm willing to take the risk? Can it afford to take the risk? Can it afford *not* to take the risk? An essential element of corporate strategic thinking must be the development of a strategy towards risk—no firm can afford the blissful ignorance of exposing itself unwittingly to unnecessarily high risk. But, of course, all firms must expose themselves to *some* risk because risk is always there in one form or another, for example:

Natural risks—death, storm, fire.

Human risks—war, riot, theft.

Technical risks—technological failure/obsolescence.

Economic risks—failure in supply or demand, inflation.

Political risks—government change, government intervention.

The object of a risk strategy is thus to clarify the magnitude of risk and to select the *degree* to which the firm will expose itself. Elements of this strategy would no doubt consider:

1 The extent to which the worst risks can be avoided by sensible selection of appropriate operational policies, e.g. limiting the number of high-risk projects undertaken at any one time.

2   The extent to which risk should be offset or insured against, e.g. some natural risks, such as fire, can be insured against; other risks can be "insured against" by offsetting or hedging operations although these can be expensive.

3   The extent to which reserves should be held to cover the risk, e.g. buffer—or safety—stocks, short-term investments, cash balances.

4   The most appropriate design for that monitoring system which will give the earliest possible warning of things beginning to go wrong.

5   The need to develop a schedule of contingent action plans that can be activated if the worst does happen (this matter will be taken further in the next chapter).

7.7   SUMMARY

The process of long-term cash forecasting can be of greater value to management than the forecast itself. This process requires the following steps:

1   Make the best guess estimate up to the planning horizon.

2   Consider what might go wrong and, thereby, prevent achievement of the best guess, and also what windfalls might permit the best guess to be surpassed.

3   Estimate how much worse or how much better it might go and thus produce a range of estimates straddling the best guess.

4   By sensitivity analysis, ascertain how critical it will be to the viability of the firm if the worst happens and it does go wrong.

5   Only if it really is critical, estimate the chances of its going wrong, i.e. ascribe subjective probabilities to the points of the range developed at (3) above.

6   Decide whether to go ahead despite the chance that things might go wrong.

7   If the decision is taken to go ahead:
      a. focus subsequent short-term forecasts and monitoring procedures so as to provide early warning of things going wrong in the danger areas;
      b. develop contingent action plans to put into operation should the worst actually happen.

This approach to the process of long-term cash forecasting will assist the firm to develop a more coherent and flexible plan which should ensure an adequacy of financial resources to meet any commitments, to seize any opportunities, and to survive any crises up to the planning horizon.

Dealing
with Financial
Emergencies

The best laid plans sometimes come unstuck!
If this should happen to the cash plan,
what can management do quickly to restore the situation
and prevent the firm from going to the wall?
There are several courses of action which could be taken
but if possible these actions should
not represent last-ditch panic measures.
Rather they should have been planned and thought through
in developing a strategy for response to potential financial emergencies.
A well-managed firm should not be "caught napping"
and in this final chapter we consider
the basic elements of this logical extension
to cash planning and strategy formulation.

8.1 THE CASE FOR FINANCIAL CONTINGENCY PLANNING

In the preceding chapter, we discussed the need to try to minimize those areas of uncertainty and risk which are associated with the future and which must somehow be taken into account when preparing a cash forecast. However, what is much more important is that if management decides to go ahead with a certain course of action, despite the reasonable probability of running some predictable risk to the continuing economic viability of the firm, then it must lay down contingency plans which can be activated should the worst happen. The 'worst' in the context of our discussion is not only insolvency but, short of insolvency, severe cash inadequacy. It is perhaps worth mentioning that cash inadequacy is not necessarily caused only by adversity but also by opportunity which, if seized, might require the immediate availability of adequate funds. If the worst does in fact happen, created either by opportunity or adversity, then what will the firm do? The ease with which this question can be answered is a very searching test of effective cash forecasting and cash control.

197

'. . .lay down contingency
plans which can be activated
should the worst happen. . .'

Many firms have an intuitive feel for what they might do in a financial
crisis, even though it is not formally thought out and written down. But this
might not be sufficiently precise to be of value to the firm in an emergency. What
is needed is an *explicit* contingency plan, rather than an *implicit* one, to deal
with financial emergencies that might arise. The reason for suggesting this is that
one of the peculiarities of financial emergencies is that unless the situation
is recognized early enough and unless appropriate remedial action is taken
quickly enough, the financial trouble can become more acute. The time lag
between the onset of a financial emergency and management's recognizing its
existence and then responding to it may be even more critical to a firm than the
onset of trouble itself. This recognition/response delay could be the killer—the
financial position might be deteriorating quickly while management is deciding what to do: remedial action must be prompt if it is to be effective.
Unfortunately, the onset of financial difficulty is not heralded with a fanfare of
trumpets. More often than not, it creeps up unannounced and, therefore, when
its presence is finally recognized it may have been festering there for some time.
By the time it is recognized, it may not be the best of times to start thinking
of remedial measures because the response mechanism that has been triggered
off may be inadequate or indiscriminate and hence even more damaging to the
firm. It may even be too late. Surely if plans to meet financial emergency have
been prepared calmly and dispassionately ahead of time, then there is greater
probability that when they are put into operation to deal with an emergency
they will represent a response which is more adequate, more appropriate, and
more timely . . . and, presumably, more successful.

The core objective of a financial contingency plan should be to reduce the
recognition/response delay in reacting to the onset of financial difficulty. The
essential elements of the plan will be:

1 Establishing appropriate means to identify the onset of financial difficulty at the earliest opportunity. In this way, the recognition delay is minimized.

2 Taking stock of all the courses of action which might be open to the firm in financial emergency.

3 Indicating the actions to be taken, by whom, when, in what sequence, and with what priority. In this way, the response delay is minimized.

8.2 EARLY IDENTIFICATION OF FINANCIAL DIFFICULTY

To get into financial difficulty is not necessarily indicative of bad management; clearly prevention is better than cure, but there are many occurrences outside the direct control of management which might precipitate financial difficulty. However, to be unable to get out of financial difficulty is much more likely to indicate bad management. We have observed above that early warning is the key to prompt and effective action by management so let us consider the steps which are necessary in order to ensure that this warning is sounded.

Effective sensitivity analysis at the planning stage will help to isolate those critical key variables upon which future financial viability rests. Because adverse movements in one or more of these key variables could trigger off a financial crisis, these variables should feature strongly in the monitoring of cash movements. The sooner information on adverse movements is available the better. Moreover, critical assumptions which have been built into the cash forecast should be monitored. Variations in these assumptions may give the earliest advance notice of forthcoming adverse cash movements or financial crises. The cost of providing this type of management information should be amply justified by the benefits that it provides to an alert management in times of crisis or impending crisis—forewarned is forearmed.

Very many "unexpected" occurrences have in fact happened before, if not to ourselves then to others in a similar position. Research into such past occurrences, like any post mortem activity, is never a pleasant occupation but, nevertheless, should provide valuable information as to a possible recurrence which might trigger off a financial crisis. Information as to the size, frequency, duration, and other characteristics of the past occurrence and as to the nature and effectiveness of remedial action taken, assist management both to recognize it and to deal with it next time around.

Many (but by no means all) financial difficulties are precipitated by national or international economic recession or depression. The behavior of a firm's cash flow in times of economic recession will be vastly different from their behavior under other difficult situations. An analysis of the firm's vulnerability to economic recession should, therefore, form part of its sensitivity analysis at the planning stage. In this context, the nature and mix of the firm's products and manufacturing facilities compared to those of its major competitors can have a critical bearing on how badly a firm will fare at times of economic recession *vis-à-vis* its competitors. What will happen to a firm's cash flow under short or prolonged bouts of economic recession? A cash flow forecast of this nature, i.e. under recession, will provide invaluable advance information to management on the need, scope, and nature of contingent action plans and might even indicate those areas where a firm might score an advantage over its competitors in times of economic recession.

Once a financial emergency arises, the situation will no doubt continue to deteriorate rapidly. Armed with advance and ongoing information on a developing financial situation, management should be able both to recognize and respond with confidence to any financial emergency—provided that potential remedial actions have been thought out and a strategy for response has been planned in advance.

8.3   TAKING STOCK OF POTENTIAL REMEDIAL ACTIONS

If financial difficulty should strike, what *can* the firm do? What actions will be available to it? What amount of cash will each action liberate? How quickly can each parcel of cash be liberated in case of need? These are the questions which management must seek to answer in taking stock, or building up a short list, of contingent action plans that can be activated should the need arise.

In Chapter 4, we discussed the monitoring and controlling of cash flow in the short term and in that chapter suggested that management's action effectively amounted to turning on the inlet valves or turning off the outlet valves of the cash tank (see Figure 2.4). Moreover, we suggested that management control action might usefully be grouped as follows:

1 *Time-related actions,* i.e. actions to bring forward cash inflows or to delay cash outflows without necessarily changing their amount.

2 *Volume-related actions,* i.e. changes in cash flow which are automatically brought about by decisions to change the volume of operations.

3 *Scale-related actions,* i.e. changes in policy relating to the degree of commitment to a specific course of action.

4 *Once-off (one-time) actions,* i.e. irreversible policy decisions creating significant, discrete, nonrecurring cash flows.

This grouping of management action can also form the framework for taking stock of potential remedial actions that will form the basis for a short list of financial contingency plans.

Time-related actions are often the easiest and least painful to apply. They represent a valuable source of cash in case of need but this source should not be squandered because its availability is limited. Frequently, timing is of the essence in reacting to a financial emergency in three respects:

1 How quickly a potential source of cash can be made available.

2 How frequently that source can be tapped.

3 For how long that particular source can be relied upon once it has been tapped.

A simple example of a potential time-related action is to delay payment to suppliers. While the amount thus liberated becomes almost immediately available, there is a limit to the number of occasions on which this can be done and similarly there is a limit to the number of months for which delay can be maintained before supplier reaction makes itself felt. On the other hand, the decision to delay a capital investment may make a larger amount of funds available once only but for as long as management decides to refrain from incurring such expenditure. One of the real dangers in not having an explicit approach to financial contingency planning and to the development of a short list of potential remedial actions is that a valuable immediate source from a time-related action might be used up without the firm's realizing it. If payment to a firm's suppliers is allowed to drift almost in automatic response to liquidity pressure, management may be unaware of the onset of the problem. By the time supplier reaction sets in and management then realizes that it is in financial difficulties, this first line of defense has gone and management must then search frantically for an alternative action which might not produce cash as quickly as is necessary. On the other hand, it would seem sensible for management consciously to initiate a time-related action, such as delaying payment to suppliers, as a means of buying time until an alternative planned course of action liberates an alternative source of cash.

Volume-related actions would normally only be considered where the financial emergency is related to declining sales. Nevertheless, these actions are always available and the cash flow consequences of all the various possibilities should be considered, for example, part-time working, percentage volume reductions, temporary suspension of production, and reliance upon subcontracted substitutions. Clearly, a number of alternatives would present themselves here and the availability of a computer model would greatly facilitate the necessary analysis.

Scale-related actions present many opportunities for economies in cash flow at times of financial difficulty. Indeed, it is a frequent and automatic reaction by many management groups to initiate cuts in budgeted levels of expenditure or to institute "economy drives." But how far should the axe be wielded and how deeply should it be allowed to cut? It is possible that indiscriminate cutting might do more harm than good. Surely, this presents yet a further justification for drawing up a short list of potential actions ahead of time. Planned scale-related actions must be more effective than indiscriminate ones, yet which manager will be prepared to admit that his or hers is the budget which carries the largest amount of fat that can be melted away in case of need? One approach to developing an acceptable management attitude towards contingent cuts in budgeted levels of expenditure is put forward by the advocates of "zero-base budgeting." A full description of this technique is beyond the scope of this book, but a brief outline might be useful. Particularly when budgeting for the provision of a service, e.g. maintenance, marketing, accounting expenditures, or inventory levels, it is common practice to start with the *status quo* and argue for the new budget from that point. Under a system of zero-base budgeting. the *status quo* is challenged and a departmental budget would periodically start at zero, that is, on the assumption that the item being budgeted was not necessary. The budget would then be built up by stages: stage 1 being the minimum considered to be worthy of the cause; stage 2 providing an improved service; stage 3 even more so; and so on up to stage N. Each stage will be more costly than the earlier stage but presumably each stage will also bring greater benefits. Management is thus in a position to assess the cost/benefit relationship of selecting a higher stage budget and is also put in the position of being able to identify acceptable levels of provision of essential services, e.g. the stage below which it cannot afford to operate; the highest stage it can afford to accept; the stages it can afford to do without. However, more importantly, the availability of multistage budgets permits management to be highly selective in indicating which departments shall be cut back, and by what amounts, should the occasion arise. This selective approach must be more effective than blindly cutting X percent off all departments irrespective of their existing stage in provision of service. The advantage to contingency planning provided by zero-based budgeting is that it creates a positive rather than a negative thought process for management—the emphasis is not on what to cut out but on the cost of providing successive department by department levels of improved service. Only in extreme emergency will the system be used as a basis for making cuts, but it will be extremely valuable in guiding management at that time into the least damaging scale-related actions.

Once-off (or one-time) actions are broadly of three types:

1 The liquidation of instant reserves held for that purpose.

2 The raising of additional funds.

3 The liquidation of surplus or redundant assets.

Instant reserves will be considered more fully later in this chapter. They are even more vital than time-related actions and must not be squandered because once used it may not be easy to restore them. The ability to raise additional funds has been discussed in an earlier chapter; clearly the type and amounts available for consideration as potential sources of cash in time of need depend upon the existing capital structure and the market and economic environment prevailing at the time. But what of the ability to liquidate assets? All firms, if they are honest, must admit that they harbor candidates for divestment—areas of the firm's activity, be they products, departments, factories, or perhaps whole divisions, the ongoing performance of which does not economically justify the continued employment of funds locked up in them. Nevertheless, there may be no better alternative use to which the funds can be put or there may be other significant nonfinancial strategic reasons why it is necessary to remain in such areas. If a firm has made the decision to remain, it would be unlikely to contemplate expansion in these areas, although it is willing to maintain its position at the lowest economic cost. However, if financial emergency befalls the firm, it may be appropriate at that time to reconsider its strategy and withdraw from these areas. Surely any strategic withdrawal should first be from the least defensible positions. For this reason, part of the art of taking stock of remedial actions, particularly in the once-off (or one-time) action area, is to undertake a rigorous analysis of all the firm's activities and to draw up a list of those activities which are not providing an adequate economic return or which can be severed from the business with the least damage to future earning potential. These are the candidates for divestment in case of need. Clearly, the funds locked up in such activities cannot be realized overnight, which underlines even more strongly the need to identify such possibilities of divestment and to think through carefully and dispassionately, well in advance of the time, what circumstances might precipitate divestment and what steps need then to be taken should it become necessary to divest.

Taking stock of potential remedial action is never easy to accomplish in practice, administratively speaking. One of the major reasons for this is that it runs counter to human nature; to many managers the mere thought of possible failure is anathema: to *plan* for it is almost disloyal to the firm. In an aura of enthusiasm and dedication to the cause, there is much more personal satisfaction in planning for success than in planning for potential failure. Planning is time consuming anyway, so if management is dedicated to success, why should it even consider potential courses of action which might be followed in the unlikely event of failure? Financial 'contingency planning can never be a popular pastime. Moreover, when knowledge gets out to lower levels of staff that a contingency planning exercise is in progress, how will this be read by them? Unfortunately there is a good possibility that it might be misread, and so set off rumors around the firm that financial difficulty is *imminent,* which of course is not the case at all. Furthermore, whom do you tell about your contingency plan? What will be their attitude if knowledge leaks out and a group of staff learns that their department is high on an assassination list to be activated and so create savings if the worst should ever happen? How do you persuade them to work their hardest and stay with the firm in the meantime? Nevertheless, management must somehow bring contingency planning out into the open and make all aware that it is necessary to seek out potential actions which can be activated if necessary to minimize the worst effects of potential future financial emergencies.

The outline reproduced in Figure 8.1 suggests a framework which might be used to schedule potential remedial actions. Notice that information is provided not only on the amount of cash flow estimated to be liberated by each action, but also the speed with which it could be liberated in case of need. The ability to select from such a schedule in case of need must help to reduce the recognition/response delay to which reference was made earlier in this chapter.

8.4 STRATEGY FOR RESPONSE

Once stock has been taken and a schedule of potential remedial actions produced, the final part of the contingency plan needs to be formulated. This is to develop a strategy for responding to financial emergencies as soon as they have been recognized. Such strategy will indicate the priorities and sequence for implementing each potential action along with the manager whose responsibility it is to give the go-ahead. It is not possible to discuss the exact form which such strategy will take in every firm, under all circumstances, because each strategy must be specific to the individual firm and to those surrounding circumstances which exist at the time of its implementation. However, it is possible to draw up some general guidelines.

The strategy must permit flexibility of implementation dependent upon the nature of the financial emergency to which it seeks to respond. Clearly, there would appear to be no pressing, immediate need to sell the factory only if a short-term crisis presented itself simply because one or two of the major customers had failed to meet their regular payment date. On the other hand, if the two major customers suddenly went out of business and it was a long haul to replace that business elsewhere, then the nature of the financial crisis is quite

	Estimated amount made available		Speed of mobilization	Length of time available
	Maximum	Minimum		

1 Liquidation of instant reserves:
    Cash and bank balances
    Short-term investments				

2 Time-related actions:
    Delay payment to suppliers
    Speed up collections from
      customers
    Delay capital expenditures
    Delay other items				

3 Volume-related actions
    Cancellation of shift
      working
    Part-time working
    Temporary closure				

4 Scale-related actions:
    Restrict revenue budgets
      Production
      Administration
      Selling
      Distribution
      R&D
    Restrict capital
      expenditures
    Reduce inventory levels
    Reduce dividend				

5 Additional sources of financing:
    Short-term borrowing
    Long-term borrowing
    Preference (or
      preferred) shares
    Equity (or common) shares				

6 Significant divestments:
    Investments in associated
      and subsidiary companies
    Undeveloped land
    Plant and equipment
    Land and buildings				

Figure 8.1

different and significant divestments might then have to be considered. As far as possible, the strategy for response to a recognized financial emergency must match the potential action to the emergency which has arisen. Each item on the list of potential remedial actions will possess certain attributes peculiar to itself, for example:

1 The degree of certainty as to the amount of cash that can be made available or mobilized—some items are completely certain, such as the realization of instant reserves of cash held on deposit at the bank; others, such as the run down and sale of a section of the business are less certain.

2 The time scale for realization of cash—some items can be mobilized more quickly than others.

3 The duration of availability of the amount of cash realized—for example, there is a limit to the amount of extension of supplier credit.

4 The dislocating impact on the future viability of the firm—some actions are relatively easier to rectify than others once the emergency has passed.

These attributes must be weighed in the balance before determining the priority with which each action will be implemented because it will be found that financial emergencies possess similar attributes also:

1 The degree of certainty as to the amount of cash required to meet the emergency.

2 The amount of advance warning given of its requirement.

3 The duration of its requirement.

4 The ability to return to normal when the emergency has passed.

If the strategy does not attempt to match the attributes of the action with those of the emergency, there is the very real danger that the line of least resistance will be followed by the firm. In this case, the order of priority for taking action would be to progress down the list looking for the action that is easiest to take or that provides the most easily realizable reserve of cash. Continuous pursuit of such a policy might result in all of the easily realizable sources of cash being mobilized and exhausted unnecessarily thereby leaving the firm particularly vulnerable if a large unexpected financial emergency presents itself. On the other hand, a strategy matching the action to the emergency would not necessarily follow the line of least resistance. For example, if information on economic trends indicates that the progress payment due in three months time on a factory currently under construction is likely to be 16 percent higher than planned, *now* is the time to implement an action that is likely to mobilize an appropriate amount of cash in three months. If, as the time draws nearer, the amount needed moves to 18 percent or the earlier action fails to generate sufficient cash soon enough, *then* could be the time to implement one of the actions that possess attributes of greater certainty as to amount of cash realizable or greater ease of mobilization.

Should there be an apparently indifferent choice among alternative courses of action to meet a given financial emergency, a sound strategist would select that course which had the least dislocating impact upon the future viability of the firm.

8.5 MAINTAINING INSTANT FINANCIAL RESERVES

A special word is necessary regarding the readily realizable instant reserve. Under what circumstances is such a tactical reserve necessary? What should be its size, in what form should it be held, and under what circumstances should it be used?

Maintenance of a reserve clearly depends upon the risk preference of management. A tactical reserve represents an insurance policy against financial emergency and the larger the reserve the lower is the risk from potential emergencies. The size of the instant reserve deemed to be necessary in any firm will be a function of the size of any expected cash deficit and the time it takes to mobilize the next most easily realizable potential source of cash. For example, if the next most easily realizable source takes 5 days to mobilize, then an instant reserve of $50,000 would provide insurance protection for an unexpected cash drain of up to $10,000 per day. However, all insurance policies bear a premium and the premium attached to a financial reserve is the loss of earnings which could have been enjoyed had the reserve been redeployed more profitably elsewhere. Clearly there must be a limit to the amount of tactical reserve that any firm can afford to carry.

The tactical reserves are available and can be called upon to meet a number of different eventualities (provided that several do not occur simultaneously). Therefore, once a reserve has been established it has multiple potential uses and clearly the economies of scale begin to be felt in determining its size; as a firm grows, its tactical reserve would not necessarily grow proportionately.

The strength of a tactical reserve is its *immediate* availability. There would seem to be no need to maintain an immediately available reserve any larger than is necessary to meet an *immediate* emergency, i.e. the one that comes completely without warning. If there is some warning of the onset of the emergency, then this warning might provide sufficient time to mobilize alternative resources. In this case, the demand for an instantly realizable reserve is consequently reduced. If the reserve is to be genuinely instantly available, it must, of course, be held only in a form that is genuinely instantly realizable. Holding actual cash fulfills this need but clearly this presents a security risk (and, perhaps, thereby also represents a potential financial emergency itself!). For this reason very short, guaranteed no-risk, investment is recommended as an alternative. Clearly, the reserve will provide little or no return if invested in this way, but this is the premium that must be paid on this particular insurance policy. If the "reserve" is invested so as to obtain an adequate return, it may not in fact be an *instant* reserve.

We have already observed earlier in this chapter that the indiscriminate and unnecessary use of the instant reserve could render the firm extremely vulnerable to a sudden and completely unexpected emergency. Ideally, the tactical reserve, as is the case with military tactical reserves, should *never* be used because the advantage of instant mobility is thereby lost: use of the instant reserve should normally represent an action of last resort. However, let us take our analogy of a military tactical reserve a stage further and follow normal military tactics. If it becomes necessary to use the instant reserve for a valid purpose, then steps should immediately be taken to restore that reserve in case a second unexpected emergency presents itself in quick succession to the first and the firm is thereby caught unprepared. There are a number of ways in which the reserve might be restored but an example will demonstrate the principle. In an extreme case, where an instant reserve has been used, it may be wise for the firm to initiate arrangements to borrow and place on deposit the funds thereby made available. In this way, the instant reserve is restored (the difference between the cost of borrowing and the amount earned on deposit now represents the new insurance premium). If the borrowing facility which has been used represents a relatively short notice and certain source of cash, then steps should be taken to repay it as soon as convenient through an action of longer term and less certain payoff, and so on until the various potential remedial actions are once more brought into balance. This permits the continuing implementation of a coherent and flexible strategy for response to future financial emergencies.

Only by a frequent inventory and scheduling of potential remedial actions is a firm able to identify the extent of its tactical instant reserves. Such an inventory may reveal a complete absence of any *immediate* reserve or a marked shortage of short-term potential actions pehaps due to the eroding effect of frequent budget cuts. If this be the case, and the firm believes it necessary to have access to such reserve, then it should consider the implementation of its less certain, more long-term actions *now,* while time is on its side, in order to restore the necessary reserve and so more fully balance its range of potential remedial actions and thereby create that degree of flexibility of action which is so vital to the firm's ability to respond immediately to a recognized crisis. As has been stated already, the recognition/response delay to a financial emergency could be more critical to the firm than the onset of the emergency itself. Time is of the essence and flexibility in response is the essence of timeliness.

Conclusion

In this book, we have attempted both to highlight the importance of cash planning, forecasting, and control and to demonstrate how management might approach this task in practice. We have no wish to overplay or to get out of perspective this particular area of management responsibility but if the ultimate objective of any business enterprise is, put in its simplest sense, to survive, then management must attempt to ensure that:

1 The firm continues as a financially viable entity and is shielded from financial shocks.

2 The firm is able to meet its debts or other financial obligations as they fall due for payment.

3 No management decision essential to the firm's existence is frustrated for lack of availability of financial resources.

4 The financial resources of the firm are deployed to the maximum economic advantage consistent with the above.

In the chapters of this book, we have suggested the following elements in management's approach to this task:

1 Create an awareness of the behavior of cash in the firm and the critical factors that determine cash flow.

2 Attempt to forecast, both in the short- and in the long-term, if, when, in what amounts, and for how long either additional cash will be required or a surplus will be available.

3 Monitor ongoing performance and initiate such remedial or control action that will, so far as is possible, improve the short-term cash position.

4 Develop that strategy toward the timely availability of additional finance which will ensure that the firm is not thereby exposed to additional risks which it would find difficult to withstand.

5 Attempt to quantify the uncertainties which surround predictions of future performance, assess the degree to which the firm's financial position might be sensitive to such uncertainties, and determine the degree of probability posed by such uncertainties to the disadvantage of the firm.

6 Evaluate what resources can be mobilized in the event of the onset of financial emergency and develop a strategy for the mobilization of such resources in case of need.

Throughout our consideration of the subject we have also repeatedly stressed the importance of the time dimension in any of the six elements listed above. Timing is one of the most critical aspects of the behavior of cash flow—an adverse movement in timing can be even more disastrous to a firm than an adverse movement in the amounts of cash flows. Management that neglects to take account of timing in any aspect of its approach to cash forecasting, planning, or control does so at its peril.

Inflation aggravates cash flow problems. In an inflation-proof economy, a firm must generate sufficient after-tax cash flow internally from current operations to provide for:

1 The replacement of resources consumed in carrying out those operations.

2 Adequate remuneration for the capital employed in carrying out those operations.

If any cash surplus remains it will help to finance expansion along with any necessary additional external capital. However, in times of inflation the cost of replacement will normally be higher than the original cost of those resources consumed. For this reason, a higher after-tax cash flow must be generated internally or the firm will be forced to seek additional external capital not to expand but simply to maintain its current position at the higher cost level. Inflation *is* growth in cash flow terms.

Index